Investing in the New Economy

James Sagner

Published by Frank J. Fabozzi Associates

© 2001 By Frank J. Fabozzi Associates
New Hope, Pennsylvania

This publication is designed to provide accurate and authoritative information in regard to the subject matter covered. It is sold with the understanding that the publisher is not engaged in rendering legal, accounting, or other professional services.

ISBN: 1-883249-98-8

Printed in the United States of America

Table of Contents

About the Author

James S. Sagner is Managing Principal of Sagner/Marks, a treasury consulting firm with offices in White Plains, NY. Prior to forming Sagner/Marks in 1992, Mr. Sagner was with the First National Bank of Chicago (now Bank One). He has managed 250 large financial studies for organizations worldwide. His clients have included leading insurance companies, securities firms, finance companies, banks, hospitals, manufacturing companies, and service organizations. He is the author of *Cashflow Reengineering* (1997) and *Financial and Process Metrics for the New Economy* (2001).

He is a faculty member in the executive education program at the University of North Carolina and the author of over 40 papers and articles that have appeared in publications such as *AFP Exchange, Corporate Cashflow*, and various other journals. He has earned a BS (Accounting), MBA, and Ph.D. (Business and Economics). Mr. Sagner, who was honored as a Rockefeller Fellow and a Beta Gamma Sigma, is a CCM and a CPCM.

Preface

Human beings depend on the apparent precision of numbers. We like to be able to add, subtract, multiply or divide quantities into neat results, and then compare those answers with other calculations to determine the best, the worst, and the average case.

When we examine a business enterprise, we look first to the things we can measure: the earnings, the sales, the assets, and the stock price. We tend to downplay the fact that a corporation is comprised of people making complex, strategic decisions about products, markets and technology, because we cannot easily "compute" these activities.

However, our focus on financial statements and quantification has become of limited value because:

- people do not appear on the balance sheet

- capital requirements diminish as non-core competencies are outsourced

- suppliers and customers make Internet offers to sell or buy

- decisions are becoming nearly real-time

- the potential for numerous unprofitable decisions is exponentially increased.

In this environment, the popular investments of the post-World War II era will be continuously challenged by aggressive, global competition. While this situation has been recognized by some critics, the emerging new economy forces open a challenge to all of our assumptions about investment analysis.

This book builds on my discussion of the corporate financial manager's e-commerce, new economy concerns in *Financial and Process Metrics for the New Economy* (Amacom Books, 2001). The timeline of discrete business activities has permitted days or weeks of time to ponder, negotiate, and decide on business deals. What's new in the 21st century environment is nearly real-time decision-making and the dramatic rise in the cost of capital. These developments demand more thoughtful consideration of revenues, costs, and profits than our five centuries-old ledger, double-entry accounting system can accommodate.

The material reviewed in that book and this volume have been greatly influenced by our experiences with Fortune 500 global corporate clients over the past two-plus decades. Through our association with these organizations, we have been able to understand the difficulties in developing useful financial information and in fostering a cooperative management climate. Unfortunately, probably not more than 15% or 20% of the large, publicly held companies are prepared for the demands of the new economy.

If you are considering becoming or currently are a stockholder, you face the potential for cataclysmic changes in the investing climate. We will show you why the old, accepted ideas will not work, and why you must alter your conception of rational stock market analysis.

Our clients have always taught us far more than we have taught them, and we are very grateful to them for their trust and confidence. Thanks to Bob Rosenthal of Salomon Smith Barney, St. Louis, for his friendship over the years. My special gratitude to Frank Fabozzi for his patience, insights, and guidance. This book is dedicated to Stephen, Amy, Robert-Paul, Jennifer, Scott, Nadya, Claire, Benjamin, and Denali.

James Sagner

Why the Financial Results Don't Matter

"If a man does not keep pace with his companions, perhaps it is because he hears a different drummer. Let him step to the music which he hears, however measured or faraway."
Henry David Thoreau, *1817-1862 (Walden, Ch. 18)*

Our attempts at evaluating companies for possible investment are largely based on various combination of quantitative information. However, such data are misleading and nearly useless as a guide to selecting stocks because of several factors:

- the numbers are misleading, as accounting data can easily be manipulated to show whatever results management chooses to announce

- any analysis has little predictive value, as the interplay of the factors chosen is complex and may represent positive or negative trends

- the data are readily available to everyone through a variety of media sources, and therefore hold no special insight for any particular investor

- senior managers of companies seldom know what is going on in their own organizations, and their statements to the financial community are for the purpose of public relations and may bear little or no relation to reality

Part I of the book reviews these issues and discusses the basis for the impending changes in the way we look at investment analysis. In Part II we will examine the prospects for specific industries and companies, in the search for the big winners, the moderate winners, and the losers. Part III will apply the concepts developed in Part II to the portfolio of a typical investor.

Chapter 1

Principles and Delusions of Stock Market Theories

October. This is one of the peculiarly dangerous months to speculate in stocks. The others are July, January, September, April, November, May, March, June, December, August and February.
Mark Twain *(Samuel Clemens), 1835-1910 (Pudd'nhead Wilson's Calendar)*

The challenge of the 21st century stock market will not be earnings, efficient markets or "technology-dot-com." The one issue which will matter for the next generation of investing is the transition of the "old" manufacturing economy to the "new" e-commerce, information economy. This book will help you locate companies which will be participants in the new economy, either through implementing or providing essential new economy strategy and technology.

Companies which implement e-commerce approaches to old economy businesses will be the big winners. Companies which provide the technology and infrastructure will be moderate winners. The rest are losers. We'll show you how to find these winners, and help develop a successful strategy to building your investment portfolio.

THE PUZZLED INVESTOR

You are Jane Smith or John Jones, are 35 or 50 years old, earning $50,000 a year, are single or married, white collar or blue collar, with or without dependents, and live in the city or in the suburbs. The principles we're going to discuss are the same for Jane or John to make them savvy investors. Jane potentially has $5,000 per year in investable funds after taxes and living expenses, which will increase as her income grows. A fairly standard rule-of-thumb in financial planning is that 10% of your annual salary should be saved/invested. Anyone over 50 years of age without significant investments should attempt to save 20% each year.

You are puzzled and perplexed by the markets: up 100 points on the Dow Jones Industrial Average one day and down 150 points the next. Your brother recommends that you buy high technology stocks. Your father, who wants to protect you, suggests utility stocks. You have some money to invest, a vague idea about your alternatives, and a need to develop an investment plan. What do you do next?

Exhibit 1-1: Future Sum of an Annuity (Selected Portion for Illustrative Purposes)

Years	10%	12%	14%	16%	18%
5	6.105	6.353	6.610	6.877	7.154
10	15.937	17.549	19.337	21.321	23.521
15	31.772	37.280	43.842	51.660	60.965
20	57.275	72.052	91.025	115.380	146.628
25	98.347	133.334	181.871	249.214	342.603
30	164.494	241.333	***356.787***	530.312	790.948

Note: Bold italics are used to indicate the compound interest factor used in the text calculation for the future value of an annual savings program.

The eventual value (or in financial terms, the "future value") of $5,000 a year invested through an assumed retirement age of 65 (a working career of 30 years from now), at 14% a year, is nearly $1.8 million before taxes, or probably about $1.5 million after the payment of some capital gains taxes[1] during the period. (The math is $5,000 times the compound interest [present value] factor for 30 years at 14% interest, 356.8. See Exhibit 1-1 for the portion of the future sum of an annuity table from which this factor is derived.)

We used 14% in this calculation as an attainable portfolio return over the past two decades. By portfolio return, we mean the average annual return for Jane's total portfolio, consisting primarily of a growth stock segment but including a small (but necessary) liquidity segment.[2] The total return (dividends and price appreciation) of the stock markets have averaged about 20% over the four year period 1996-1999, and exceeded 18% in the decade of the 1990s.[3] The amount Jane will have available to invest should increase with her increasing earnings power. As the result, she could have a substantial portfolio by age 65.

The Purpose of Investing

Why does Jane need to amass $1.5 million by the time she retires? Jane cannot depend on Social Security for any significant help in maintaining her lifestyle, although government payments will likely provide a minimal level of support. Her pension from her employer should be more substantial — provided she keeps her job. However, the job security of the American worker has been severely threatened in the past decade, and job changes and periods of unemployment are unfortunate possibilities.

Jane will likely live another 40 or more years, and may have to care for her aging parents. If she marries, there could be significant child rearing

---

[1] "Capital gains" arise from the sale of investment property which has appreciated in value. Such gains are subject to preferential tax treatment.

[2] We will discuss the construction of Jane's portfolio in Part III.

[3] For large company stocks, the 1980s average was 17.5%. See *Stocks, Bonds, Bills and Inflation, 2000 Yearbook*, Ibbotson Associates, 2000, Table 1-1, p. 19.

expenses. Assuming that she will need $50,000-$60,000 for her living costs, Jane will require about $80,000 per year in post-retirement income. A $1.5 million portfolio will throw off nearly $100,000 if conservatively invested at 6.5%, a prudent strategy once the prime earnings years are over. Any unusual living costs such as hospitalization could easily consume the safety margin between $80,000 and $100,000. It is clear that Jane cannot be passive if she wants to assure her financial security later.

The central issue is: how will Jane attain a 14% annual return?

- She can't do it using *government or corporate bonds*, as current interest rates are 5.15% for 10-year U.S. Treasury notes and 5.5% for 30-year Treasury bonds, and about 6.5% for investment grade corporate bonds.

- She may be able to do it in *real estate* or such collectibles as *fine arts and gold*, but fortunes have been lost in certain sectors of these markets. Besides, such "hard" assets are not liquid and have huge transaction costs, such as broker commissions, attorney fees, documentation costs, auctioneer costs, etc.

- Stocks are the only liquid, relatively safe investment possibility. However, should she invest using mutual funds, her broker's recommendations, or make her own decisions?

The only way Jane will meet her target return is through the search for investments in e-commerce, new economy companies, because their returns will exceed the average returns of all stocks. To understand the "why's" and "how's," Jane (and you) will have to read the rest of this book.

BASIC APPROACHES TO STOCK MARKET INVESTING

The three basic stock market investment approaches are fundamental analysis, technical analysis and the efficient market theory.

- *Fundamental analysis* studies the underlying economic and business potential of the company, its industry and/or the economy.

- *Technical analysis* looks at volume, diversity and a number of other factors as predictors of future stock price action.

- The *efficient market hypothesis* assumes that all knowledge about stocks is available to investors as public information, and that future stock prices cannot be predicted.

Fundamental and technical analyses and the efficient market hypothesis (EMH) are now so establishment that most of the larger stock brokerage firms have hired staff of analysts in each "discipline".

However, any time an idea about the stock market becomes widely accepted, its predictive value becomes marginal due to anticipation of the next bit of economic news, the next crossing of a technical resistance level or the next analysis of systematic risk. These approaches are of limited value in a 21st century investing environment. In this chapter we'll see why, and the chapters which follow we'll offer our alternative.

Fundamental Analysis

The underlying basis of fundamental analysis is that company earnings results and future potential is the primary determinant of the price of a stock, as most commonly measured by earnings per share (EPS). The fundamental analyst searches for the correct "intrinsic value" of a stock based on estimates of future earnings, dividends and other key economic and financial indicators. The current stock price is then compared to the intrinsic value in the search for an undervaluation, which is a buying opportunity.

Benjamin Graham and David Dodd are considered as the most influential fundamental analysts or value investors; their seminal contribution *Security Analysis* (1934) is discussed in Chapter 3. Critical to this work is the use of a company's financial statements to develop earnings projections after careful examination of and any necessary adjustments to the company's accounting practices.

The most common driver of modern fundamental analysis is the price-earnings ratio (P/E), where a fair price of a stock is derived from projected EPS times a multiplier (the P/E) based on P/Es for companies in that same industry with similar characteristics. Most fundamental analyses begin with macroeconomics, which involves the evaluation of general economic activity, interest rates, job creation, the position of the dollar against other world currencies, the U.S. balance of payments and trade position, the federal budget deficit, and a host of other factors.

Although intuitively appealing, fundamental analysis has the flaw of a dependence on accounting reports, such as earnings per share. These data do not reflect the quality of earnings, pressures on management, new initiatives, actions by competitors or other non-accounting data. Furthermore, they may be incorrect or misleading, in that accounting rules govern the treatment of certain assets (such as inventory FIFO or LIFO treatment, and the depreciation method used for plant and equipment).[4]

---

[4] The annual cost of any asset with a life exceeding one year must be annually expensed, and cannot be deducted in the year of acquisition. There are various acceptable depreciation methods in common use, including straight-line, sum-of-the-years digits and double declining balance. Inventory may be costed as first-in, last-out (FIFO); last-in, first-out (LIFO); or average cost. For an explanation, consult any standard accounting text.

These data problems persist even in the application of quantitative modeling techniques by portfolio managers to investment decisions. For example, "factor models" use company, industry and market data to determine factors which correlate with stock returns. The analyst attempts to manage risk exposure and avoid unintended stock bets by pinpointing specific variations from a specified benchmark, such as the Standard & Poor's (S&P) 500 stock index. While the statistical methods are valid, the data remain of suspicious reliability.

There is no inherently predictive component within fundamental analysis, in that past performance is used to evaluate the future potential of the stock price. In fact, that future price or intrinsic value may never be recognized by the market. Or, the intrinsic value may be wrong, as the analyst may use incorrect valuation methods.

Everything that is publicly known about the company is available to everyone, and so the stock price already reflects all economic and company data. Fundamental analysis requires the investor essentially to extrapolate what is known to what may happen to a stock's price based on future earnings, dividends, interest rates and other factors. However, an important element in the price of a stock isn't even formally considered by fundamental analysts: market psychology, or the premium or discount paid for future earnings at any point in a market cycle.

Technical Analysis

Technical analysis uses the statistics of market activity to predict the movement of stock prices, including the interpretation of the supply and demand chart patterns of the past performance of a stock. The basic premise of technical analysis (or charting) is that a study of what other investors are doing, by a careful observation of market statistics, will allow the prediction of future crowd behavior. Technical analysis is therefore explicitly psychological in its approach to anticipating the actions of investors.

Earnings expectations are unimportant to a technician, on the assumption that the current price of a stock fully reflects those expectation by the market's action of continuous adjustment to new data. Instead of using macroeconomics or company-specific information, technical analysis uses the dynamic interaction of various market statistics to predict future stock prices. These include:

- support and resistance levels for the price of a stock (or its 30, 60 or 200 day moving average)

- point and figure charts showing up and down stock patterns (but not correlated to time patterns)

- measures of volume and breadth (or advance-decline)

- relative strength/weakness indicators of stocks out- or underperforming the market or the industry

- contrarian statistics (data used to determine the general trend so as to invest in the opposite position)

Various studies have been conducted of technical analysis, demonstrating that the use of stock or market activity statistics cannot predict future stock price behavior. Drawing simple lines between a stock's recent prices, or a moving average of those prices, does not consistently indicate the future direction in a stock price.

Technicians have constructed an elaborate nomenclature to explain deviations from basic trends, including head and shoulder patterns, flag formations and teacups with handles, and the reverse of each of these, with rationalizations for every variation and twitch. However, these explanations and forecasts have been shown to be random events, lacking the capability of predicting the next price change.

THE EFFICIENT MARKET HYPOTHESIS

The efficient market hypothesis (EMH) claims that it is futile to predict stock performance and that the future direction of stock prices is a "random walk". Indeed, one of the most popular books on the EMH is Burton Malkiel's *A Random Walk Down Walk Street*.[5] Two strategies are used by proponents of the EMH:

- Buy and hold those stocks which represent a broad market index (such as the S&P 500 stock index, or a mutual fund which is "indexed" to that market average, to match (but not beat) the performance of the market; *or*

- Build a portfolio representing the degree of risk that the investor will accept. This risk is called the Beta, the systematic risk of individual stocks or portfolios of stocks to changes in the general market. Beta is measured by the historic movement of a stock relative to a broad market index, usually the S&P 500 index.

A Beta of 0.0 means that the portfolio or investment is risk free, as with U.S. Treasury obligations. There is essentially no risk that the U.S. government will default on its outstanding debt. A Beta of 1.0 means that the stock will change in the same proportion as the market (usually measured as the S&P 500). A 20% rise in the market should therefore mean a 20% increase in the price of the stock. An example of a stock with a Beta of 1.0 is IBM. A Beta of 1.5 means that a 20% market rise or decline should affect the stock's price by 30%. An example of a stock with a Beta of 1.5 is The Gap retail stores.

The 30-year Treasury bond (0.0 Beta) pays about 5.5% (in early 2001), and the market return (1.0 Beta) is about 14%, comprised of a dividend return and

---

[5] W.W. Norton & Co. (7th edition), 1999.

a growth return, derived from an increase in the price of the stock. As risk (as measured by Beta) increases, the required return rises to compensate the investor for the higher risk level. A risk (Beta) level of 2.0 will require a return of over 20%; that is, the expected total return from dividends and growth would have to exceed 20% to attract investors.

The construction of a portfolio involves the selection of stocks which will reflect the desired risk profile of the investor on a dollar-weighted basis, as calculated by multiplying the Beta times the number of shares times the market price of the stock. A portfolio Beta of 1.5 could be attained by buying The Gap; or with two stocks in equal dollar amounts with Betas of 1.25, such as the insurer Allstate, and 1.75, such as Tellabs, the voice and data equipment company; or by buying any number of stocks with a dollar weighted Beta of 1.5. We will revisit the concept of Beta in the capital allocation decision-making in Chapter 9.

Is the Market a Random Walk?

The efficient market hypothesis is intellectually appealing, and is now the basis of much of the academic literature in our business schools. However, if the EMH were correct, no investor could consistently find stocks to outperform the market unless levels of market risk are accepted which are greater than market risk. In other words, it would be fruitless to search for stocks to beat the market, and the only rational approaches would be either to construct a portfolio representing an acceptable risk level, or to invest in mutual funds with holdings consistent with the designated risk profile.

However, there clearly are investors who have successfully outperformed the markets at reasonable risk levels, as profiled in such publications as *Business Week* and *Fortune*, various books, and such television shows as *Wall Street Week with Louis Rukeyser* (PBS). Each guru has a particular approach to stock market success using his own concept of fundamental analysis, such as value investing (often attributed to Warren Buffett) or "bottom-up" analysis (credited to Peter Lynch and Julian Robertson). The approaches of some of the better known and successful investors are profiled in Appendix 1.

The EMH is an interesting concept, but one which has been beaten numerous times. Recent research supports this conclusion, finding that investment style-adjusted mutual fund managers repeated their superior performance with enough consistency to refute the concept of an efficient stock market.[6]

Are Markets Rational?

Moreover, the basic premise in the EMH is that the stock market reflects all available economic and company information. Stocks and market averages should only change to the extent that new information is received by investors. How then can the theory

---

[6] See Roger Ibbotson, "Do Winning Mutual Funds Repeat?" *TMA Journal*, November/December 1996, pp. 50-56.

explain the 500 point drop (or more than 20%) in one day's trading (on October 19, 1987), to under 1800 as measured by the Dow Jones Industrial Average (DJIA)?

Certainly no event occurred at that time to justify such a decline. There were disturbances, including a rise in yields on long-term U.S. government bonds, a threatened "merger tax" from Congress, and talk of encouraging the decline of the U.S. dollar. None of these events were of a sufficient threat to explain a one day decline of over 20% unless you assume that all sellers perceived the bearish nature of this data at the *same* time.

More rational explanations of wild market fluctuations include market psychology and program trading as likely causes. Behavioral finance assumes that psychology is an important component in stock market activity. Investors are motivated by fear, hope, overconfidence, and the need for short-term gratification.[7]

"Program trading" is the issuance of buy/sell orders by computer when a stock's price or a market average crosses certain price points. The New York Stock Exchange is so concerned with the effect of program trading that it has imposed trading limits whenever the DJIA advances or declines more than a pre-established amount in a single trading day.

Why the 21st Century Will Be Different

Fundamental and technical analysis were developed in the first half of the 20th century, and the EMH in the early 1970s. The three approaches to stock analysis were successful for some period of time, until there was general and widespread understanding of their methodology. Once the markets accepted each approach and used it in stock evaluation, the theory no longer had any real usefulness in forecasting stock prices.

Business and economic information is instantly and widely available to the investment community through such sources as television (*e.g.*, CNBC, CNN, etc.), the Internet, radio business news broadcasts, portable stock quote machines, and other electronic media. By the time you are reading tomorrow's *Wall Street Journal* with its reports on today's news, that news is out of date.

Any thought that you can seize business data and analyze it before the markets do is absurd. Stock prices adjust up and down to any actual or anticipated news, so that the use of fundamental and technical analyses to beat the market is a futile exercise. The EMH assumes that you can't beat the market, although specific investors do it all the time. Can you? Keep reading!

WHAT DOES THIS ALL MEAN TO THE INVESTOR?

In this chapter we have established that the three accepted approaches to stock market analysis will not be of much help if Jane Smith is to meet her target 14%

---

[7] See, for example, Hersh Shefrin, *Beyond Greed and Fear: Understanding Behavioral Finance and the Psychology of Investing*, Harvard Business School Press, 1999.

return. Fundamental analysis won't help her as public business and company information is universally known almost instantly, and is factored into stock prices on a real-time basis. Technical analysis won't help her as there never has been a proven relationship between price and volume mechanics and future stock prices. The EMH won't help her as it simply isn't true that stocks are a random walk and that current prices reflect everything known.

Jane will not be able to read about other forms of investments in this book, such as real estate, precious metals, 19th century paintings and coins. There are experts who should be consulted regarding those alternatives. However, most investment advisors strongly recommend financial assets, such as stocks and bonds, over "hard" assets, such as gold and artwork, given their proven returns over many decades, their liquidity and low transaction costs, and the relative stability of the equity and debt markets. A few words are in order regarding the other financial asset — bonds — before we close this chapter.

The most prominent driver of changes in bond prices as measured by interest rates and yield curve relationships is market inflationary expectations. As evidence develops regarding consumer and wholesale prices, the markets continually assume that the Federal Reserve Board will react with changes in short-term rates. You should keep your eye on the factors of production as the critical components of prices: raw materials, labor and the cost of money.

Commodities prices account for less than 10% of costs in the economy, and such prices typically rise or fall within a short time frame. At the present time, there is no compelling evidence of a permanent increase in raw materials prices. Economists have varying opinions on wages, but many believe that structural factors supporting inflationary pay increases are weak: union membership is low, downsizing continues, and many employed workers are underemployed, effectively increasing the real rate of unemployment.

A real fear is the cost of money, related to long-term interest rates and to the relative strength of the dollar. If rates do rise, the dollar will strengthen even further, seriously affecting exports and the nation's balance of payments. The Fed is well aware of the difficult competitive position this would create for American companies, and will be reluctant to exacerbate the current strength of the dollar.

With the factors of production in relative stability, long-term interest rates may be about as high as they will go. This situation strongly suggests that the upward bias in stock market prices will continue for an extended period, despite years like 2000 when the stock market fell about 9%. This makes investments in bonds relatively unattractive.

The Bull Market

There are other factors driving the long-term bull market:

- *Individual Investing.* There is a growing perception that traditional retirement savings plans, such as pensions and Social Security, will not be available or adequate to support retirees. Warnings about the illiquidity of Social Security sometime in the next 20 years are generally accepted as fact by many workers, and there is concern that unfunded pension obligations or a downsized corporate America may limit retirement expectations. These anxieties are driving massive stock market investment, both directly through brokers and indirectly through mutual fund purchases.

- *Changes in Traditional Valuation Methods.* P/Es and other market and stock measurements have long provided valuation rules which have proven useless in the current economic climate. Two examples from the 1997-early 2000 stock market boom:

  - "Dividend yields below 3% are too low for the stock market to sustain." This rule is not very useful with yields at 2% and many observers wondering why an investor would prefer a dividend payment, with its double taxation problem, to a capital gains tax in some future year. (The "double taxation" of dividends derives from the fact that dividends, unlike interest expenses, are *not* deductible to companies in the calculation of taxable income. Furthermore, they are taxable to individuals as ordinary income.)

  - "P/Es at about 20 times are at the high end of the traditional range, which would also appear to make stock prices unsustainable at recent levels." However, earnings are subject to various accounting interpretations which have nothing to do with economic realities; see Chapter 3.

Thus, the traditional red flags to sell stocks in early 2000 were being ignored.

What This Book Does Not Do

There are two things this book does not do. First, no formal procedure or discussion is provided on procedures for macroeconomic analysis. Many investment books devote significant amounts of space to the general business climate, the evaluation of economic conditions, interest rate, inflation and the position of the U.S. dollar in the global economy.

This book assumes that the long economic cycle is positive, with major market averages moving generally higher although corrections will inevitably occur. However, although a declining market would adversely affect nearly any investment, the stocks we will be discussing would be good candidates to perform satisfactorily.

Second, this book is not a primer or introductory text on the stock market, nor does it review other types of investments. Investment books come in all shades and variation, discussing retirement, bankruptcy, wills and estates, insurance, real estate, precious metals, foreign tax havens, and general money management including budgeting. This book only discusses the stock market and stock selection.

We have already used a number of phases and terms the meaning of which may not be obvious to the new investor: the Federal Reserve Board (or Fed), references to inflation, various types of interest rates, mutual funds, double taxation of dividends, etc. This book assumes that the reader is familiar with these concepts, and proceeds with the presentation of the ideas of the book without pausing to define or explain them.

It is strongly suggested that the newer investor study any of the excellent basic books on investing available in your bookstore or library before investing any money. Never buy a stock (or anything else) on a tip; make sure you understand what you're buying and that the financial service company representative is with a reputable firm.

Chapter 2

What Financial Statements Reveal and What They Conceal

When you can measure what you are speaking about, and express it in numbers, you know something about it; but when you cannot measure it ... your knowledge is of a meager and unsatisfactory kind: it may be the beginning of knowledge, but you have scarcely, in your thoughts, advanced to the stage of science.
Lord Kelvin, *1824-1907 (physicist and astronomer)*

Choosing a stock essentially involves the investigation of a company to try to determine its viability as an investment. There are things we can examine and things we cannot examine. For example, we can review the financial statements — the income statement and the balance sheet — and the narrative commenting on the past year's operations, all of which are printed in the annual report. We can compare the company to others in its industry using various published sources. All of these data are historical, in that they dutifully report on the results of the past year based on generally accepted accounting standards.

We cannot get the critical data we would like to have to really understand the company, such as sales prospects, profits by product line, customer complaints and quality problems, and products under development. Management has an idea of its prospects for the coming years and of its current problems, and we can guess as to the impact of coming events. However, published forecasts of earnings vary fairly widely, and can be well off actual results.

This chapter discusses what company financial information reveals and what is concealed by examining measures commonly used in stock market analysis. What is revealed will not prove to be very helpful, and possibly downright misleading, and what is concealed is critically important in any thoughtful analytical process. We begin with absolute dollar calculations, such as working capital, and then briefly examine cash budgeting, discounted cash flow analysis, and the various significant ratios used to compare financial statement accounts. We conclude with general reasons that these various measures are inadequate, and a comment on qualitative commentary and analysis.

TRADITIONAL FINANCIAL MEASURES

Restrictions on access to data limit the investor to the analysis of a company's performance based on certain traditional financial measures. To make this a "live" discussion, we'll being using Hewlett-Packard (HWP[1]), a company that has been prominently noted for the past two decades for superior products. The measures used include ratio analysis and the absolute dollar calculations "working capital," "cash flow," and "book value," and are illustrated using HWP data from 1995.

Working Capital

Working capital is calculated as current assets less current liabilities. Decisions regarding working capital management are usually based on the matching of the maturity of each element, as a conscious attempt is made to structure the need for cash (current liabilities) with access to cash (current assets). This need for cash is known as "liquidity."

However, working capital is a single number comprised of current account items which may be very liquid or lacking liquidity, such as cash and accounts payable; somewhat liquid, such as receivables; and of questionable liquidity, such as stale inventory. As such, merely knowing that HWP's working capital position is $5.3 billion is not very useful to the investor. All that this tells us is that there is $5+ billion more currently available *if* all assets can be turned into cash.

If half of HWP's inventory were stale and if half of receivables were uncollectible, working capital would be negative. (We are not suggesting that either is the case for HWP; remember, this is just an illustration.) Since we cannot examine the receivables or the inventory, we have no way of determining the true working capital number.

Cash Flow

Cash flow was traditionally calculated somewhat simplistically as net income plus any non-cash expense, such as depreciation or amortization. Current usage refines the definition to "EBITDA," or earnings before interest, taxes, depreciation and amortization. "Free cash flow" is EBITDA less dividend payments to stockholders, to show cash available for debt repayment.

EBITDA shows the amount of cash actually derived from the ongoing operations of a business. It corrects for the accrual accounting convention of depreciating assets over their useful life even though the cash required for the purchase was expended at the beginning of the life of the project. Cash flow is considered as more indicative of the company's cash production capacity than balance sheet "cash."

Cash flow is important as it is *the* source of dividends and internally generated equity capital (also called "retained earnings"), rather than by the sale of new stock. However, because cash flow may be used for either of these purposes,

---

[1] HWP is the New York Stock Exchange (NYSE) symbol for Hewlett-Packard.

or for the repurchase of securities previously issued, the determination of a single number does not provide much informational content to the investor.

This is because it is not known whether the company has a good use for the cash, or if cash is insufficient, or whether external sources are available (such as bank loans). We know that HWP's cash flow was $3.6 billion in fiscal year 1995; we don't know what HWP's management planned to do with that cash or whether it was enough to meet the company's needs.

Book Value

Book value is calculated as total assets less total liabilities, and is often presented as "book value per share" by dividing book value by the number of common stock shares outstanding. Book value per share is then compared to a stock's market price, and conclusions are drawn as to whether the stock is worth more or less than the marketplace believes. For example, in late 1996, HWP was selling for a market price between $50 and $55 with a book value of $11.61 (based on the 1995 financial statements).

Obviously, the stock price far exceeds the book value, but what does this mean? Is the stock overpriced? Investors apparently are buying HWP's marketing expertise, dominant position in the computer printer business, the intellectual capability of its employees, and other attributes not found on the balance sheet. Book value may have some meaning in certain situations, but its use is extremely limited.

Cash Budgeting

The cash budget projects the monthly cash position, using historical patterns to forecast receipt and disbursement activity. The objective of this procedure is to determine if the company has sufficient cash to meet its expected cash needs for ongoing transactions, while providing adequate funds for contingencies. While the typical investor does not have the necessary data to determine if the company has adequate cash, stock analysts often have access to historical data to enable such scrutiny.[2]

To illustrate cash budgeting, let's look at a company with net sales of $30 million in May, $20 million in June, $30 million in July, and $25 million in August. Its cash collections are 25% the month of the sale, 65% in the month after the sale, and 10% in the second month after the sale.

Purchases are limited to 75% of that month's sales (paid during that month to maintain vendor relations), and payroll is fixed at $2 million each month. The cash position at the beginning of July is $6 million, and the desired level of cash is $5 million. This simplified scenario produces the cash budget shown in Exhibit 2-1.

---

[2] A recent example was the analysis of the "burn" rate of publicly traded Internet stocks, which concluded that 25% will exhaust their cash within one year. See, Jack Willoughby, "Burning Up," *Barron's* (March 20, 2000), pp. 29-32.

Exhibit 2-1: Simplified Cash Budget (dollars in millions)

	May	June	July	August
Sales	$30.0	$20.0	$30.0	$25.0
Collections				
25% Month of sale	$7.5	$5.0	$7.5	$6.3
65% Month After Sale	#	$19.5	$13.0	$19.5
10% 2nd Month After Sale	#	#	$3.0	$2.0
Receipts			$23.5	$27.8
Purchases			($17.5)	($20.9)
Payroll			($2.0)	($2.0)
Net Cash Activity			$4.0	$4.9
Beginning cash			$6.0	$10.0
Ending cash			$10.0	$14.9

\# - Earlier months of sales data not provided

Exhibit 2-2: Calculation of DCF of Hewlett-Packard Stock (as of late 1996)

Cash Flow by Year	PV Factor	Dividend/Stock Price Estimates	FV of Dividends and Stock Price
1997 Dividend	0.769	$0.50	$0.38
1998 Dividend	0.675	$0.55	$0.37
1999 Dividend	0.592	$0.60	$0.35
2000 Dividend	0.519	$0.65	$0.33
2000 Stock Price Estimate	0.519	$100.00	$51.90
Total			$53.33

This cash budget analysis suggests that there is ample cash available during the company's July and August period, and that there may be an opportunity by August to invest nearly $10 million in surplus cash. The only problem with these conclusions is that they don't take into account intra-month variations, which can be fairly significant. The company which relies solely on a monthly cash budget may be overdrawn at the bank (and embarrassed!) on particular days during the month.

Discounted Cash Flow Analysis

Discounted cash flow (or DCF) uses present value to calculate the "fair" current value of future earnings or dividends. "Present value" (PV) is the value today of a dollar received or spent in the future. The analyst might forecast the dividend stream out to Year 5, the expected value of the company at the end of the forecast period, and an interest rate, adjusted for risk using Beta (see Chapter 1), at which these amounts are discounted back to the present.

For example, Value Line estimated HWP's dividends for 1997 at 50¢ per share, and for the year 2000 at 65¢ per share. Their price target for 2000 was $100. With a Beta of 1.15, the discount rate used in a DCF analysis would be 14%. The current "fair" value of HWP would be calculated as $53.33, which was close to the price as of the end of 1996. The calculation is shown in Exhibit 2-2.

This is a seriously flawed process, as it assumes the amount of future earnings, the percentage of those earnings that will be paid as dividends, and the discount rate used in the computation. Corporate financial managers use present value to calculate the net present value (NPV) or internal rate of return (IRR) for capital budgeting projects.[3] They constantly find that assumptions about interest rates and cash flows are incorrect. As the result, projects which seem quite attractive today prove to be disasters by Year 5. The same is likely to be true of stocks recommended based on DCF analysis.

WHAT ARE RATIOS?

Ratio analysis was developed in the 1920s to assist in the measurement of financial performance. Among the publishers of financial information, Dun & Bradstreet, Robert Morris Associates, and Value Line compute significant ratios. Ratios measure various categories of performance by comparing various balance sheet and income statement entries.

These services all publish various types of ratios for the median (or middle case) in each industry groupings. In addition, ratios are calculated for the first quartile (25th percentile) and third quartile (75th percentile), on the theory that this is the "normal" range of experience within the industry. (There are four quartiles or 100 percentiles in any array of numbers.)

It is assumed that the first through the third quartile represent "normal" performance. Ratios demonstrating normal results are accepted without concern for possible adjustments or improvements. Results lying outside of the interquartile range may be considered as unacceptable and worthy of corrective action. For example, a current ratio of less than 1.0 is often thought of as too low to be "safe."

We'll discuss the types of ratios, problems in their interpretation and provide illustrations using HWP. In each case, HWP's results are shown in the upper box, and the industry's ratios for the third quartile, median and first quartile are shown in the lower box. HWP ratios which are outside of the normal range are shown in boldface.[4]

Liquidity or Solvency Ratios

We noted earlier that "liquidity" (or "solvency") is a term referring to the cash position of a business, and its ability to meet obligations or debts as they come due for payment. "Cash" refers to actual cash in the bank or in short-term investments, to expected cash from receipts for invoices to customers or other sources, and to credit arrangements with banks or other lenders. Liquidity ratios measure this cash (but not in-place

---

[3] A "time value of money" calculation is a standard measure of the interest rate equivalent of the in- and outflows of a capital project, computed as a dollar amount (the net present value) or as an interest rate (the internal rate of return) which is compared to a company's cost of funds (the "cost of capital"). See any standard corporate finance book.

[4] All industry data is from *1995 Industry Norms & Key Business Ratios*, Dun & Bradstreet, for SIC 3571, electronic computers, industry assets over $50 million, p. 489.

loan agreements), and are considered as critical to the integrity of a business in the measurement of whether a business can pay its bills. If debts cannot be paid, the business could be put into bankruptcy by its creditors.

The two most important liquidity measures are the *current ratio* and the *quick ratio* (or *acid test ratio*). The current ratio is calculated from balance sheet accounts, by the division of current assets by current liabilities.

- Current assets are generally defined as assets which will be turned into cash within the period of a year, such as accounts receivable, inventory, and short-term investments.

- Current liabilities are considered as debts which must be paid within one year, such as accounts payable or notes payable.

The quick ratio uses current assets, but deducts inventory in the calculation, on the theory that it is unlikely to be worth 100% of its cost in the event of a forced liquidation to pay current liabilities. The formula for the quick ratio is (Current Assets − Inventory) or (Cash + Accounts Receivable) ÷ Current Liabilities.

Other liquidity ratios include current liabilities-to-net worth, current liabilities-to-inventory, total liabilities-to-net worth, and fixed assets-to-net worth. All four of these ratios (see Exhibit 2-3) determine the ability of the company to meet short or long-term obligations as compared to industry averages.

HWP's liquidity ratios show "normal" results except for fixed assets-to-net worth, with the company having a greater percentage of fixed assets than its peer group. Dun & Bradstreet might claim that this is undesirable as HWP's working capital position may be too low, or that too much debt has been incurred to fund operations. However, there is no other indication that HWP has too much debt (for example, see the Total Liabilities-to-Net Worth Ratio) or too little working capital (see the Current and Quick Ratios).

Exhibit 2-3: Liquidity Ratios

HWP's Liquidity Ratios	1995	1994	1993
Quick Ratio (times)	0.9	0.9	1.09
([Current Assets − Inventory]) ÷ Current Liabilities	1.6/1.1/0.7	1.3/1.0/0.6	1.8/1.3/0.9
Current Ratio (times)	1.5	1.5	1.5
(Current Assets ÷ Current Liabilities)	2.6/1.9/1.4	2.3/1.8/1.3	2.8/2.1/1.4
Current Liabilities ÷ Net Worth (%)	92.4%	82.9%	80.7%
	37.1/78.5/117.9	47.9/80.7/134.2	41.9/57.6/127.4
Current Liabilities ÷ Inventory (%)	182.0%	192.6%	164.2%
	132.9/236.8/288.3	134.2/243.3/348.0	109.4/171.3/300.6
Total Liabilities ÷ Net Worth (%)	98.0%	88.4%	88.5%
	51.9/98.4/175.8	56.9/110.0/158.9	56.9/86.1/186.5
Fixed Assets ÷ Net Worth (%)	**69.2%**	**71.1%**	**76.4%**
	23.8/32.0/49.2	**22.2/34.9/60.4**	**21.9/28.7/49.1**

The problem with the use of liquidity ratios is that they only measure the ability of a company to pay its bills. In fact, they assume the worst case, that assets must be liquidated to satisfy creditors. They do not measure the ability of a company to generate earnings, usually considered as the principal driver of the stock price.

Activity or Efficiency Ratios

Measures of activity or efficiency compare balance sheet and income statement accounts, to determine the effectiveness of management's use of its resources. Such measures include:

- *Inventory Turnover*, calculated as sales divided by inventory. The theory of this ratio is that inventory turnover should be at a high enough rate to generate earnings, and not sit idle awaiting sales or disposal. Various problems arise with inventory turnover, including the comparison of a sales number with a cost number (inventory), which muddles the meaning of the result. Furthermore, many businesses experience inventory cycles, often due to seasonality, making the calculation of a ratio at any given moment in time potentially meaningless.

- *Average Collection Period*, calculated as accounts receivable divided by sales per day. This ratio measures the number of days required to collect receivables arising from credit sales. The average collection period is theoretically sound, that is, the calculation of collection days makes sense and is useful in determining whether the company's credit and collection efforts are sufficiently aggressive. However, it has effectively no meaning in stock selection.

- *Fixed Asset Turnover*, calculated as sales divided by fixed assets (net of accumulated depreciation), and *Total Assets Turnover*, calculated as sales divided by total assets. The intent of these ratios is to measure how productive plant and equipment and other fixed assets, and total assets, are in the generation of sales. Supposedly, low total or fixed asset turnover indicates inefficient use of assets.

  However, the 21st century corporation depends heavily on resources which are not even measured on the balance sheet, such as innovation, people, and systems. Besides, companies are frequently encumbered with equipment which becomes technologically obsolete long before depreciation rules permit its write-off. A good example is a personal computer with a memory capacity or a processing chip of a previous generation.

Other activity ratios include total assets-to-sales, sales-to-net working capital, and accounts payable-to-sales.

HWP's activity ratios (see Exhibit 2-4) show divergent results, with sales-to-inventory below the normal range (in 1995) but sales-to-working capital above that range (in 1995 and 1994). Dun & Bradstreet might claim that sales are strained from overuse of working capital; however, since inventory is part of working capital, the activity ratios should probably be ignored. This group of ratios are not supportive of the needs of stock market investing, although they do provide useful detail on the average collection period and possibly other transaction components. As we have seen in the HWP example, the overall results are not terribly meaningful.

Profitability Ratios

All profitability ratios measure earnings (or net profits after taxes), using sales, assets, net working capital, and net worth as the most common units of comparison. We will be discussing earnings in some detail in Chapter 3.

HWP's results (see Exhibit 2-5) far exceed those of its industry. In the case of the profitability ratios, Dun & Bradstreet does not criticize results above the normal range!

The Use and Misuse of Ratio Analysis

Ratio analysis can warn investors and creditors about possible problems, but those possible problems can also be indications of an aggressive business.

- Is a Current Ratio of less than 1.0 (or 1.4 for the computer industry) too low to be "safe"?

Exhibit 2-4: Activity Ratios

HWP's Activity Ratios	1995	1994	1993
Collection Period (days)	78.0	73.4	79.4
(Accounts Receivable ÷ Sales Per Day)	65.5/84.0/99.3	66.4/76.7/96.7	57.2/87.2/106.5
Sales ÷ Inventory (times)	**5.2**	5.8	6.6
	9.6/7.8/5.5	10.4/8.0/4.9	10.0/6.9/5.6
Total Assets ÷ Sales (%)	77.5%	78.3%	82.4%
	71.0/90.9/125.6	65.6/82.7/104.7	70.6/88.0/105.8
Sales ÷ Working Capital (times)	**6.0**	**5.8**	6.0
	5.6/3.5/2.3	**5.6/4.2/2.5**	7.5/3.1/1.9
Accounts Payable ÷ Sales (%)	7.7%	5.9%	**4.1%**
	6.7/8.9/13.5	5.6/7.3/9.4	**6.5/7.9/12.8**

Exhibit 2-5: Profitability Ratios

HWP's Profitability Ratios	1995	1994	1993
Return on Sales (%)	**7.7%**	**6.4%**	5.8%
	6.3/3.2/(2.1)	**6.0/(0.4)/(5.5)**	7.0/1.2/(4.3)
Return on Assets (%)	**11.1%**	**8.8%**	7.7%
	8.5/5.0/1.4	**7.1/(0.5)/(7.4)**	9.9/0.9/(4.6)
Return on Net Worth (%)	**22.4%**	**17.3%**	14.7%
	16.9/12.4/3.7	**13.0/2.2/(16.5)**	14.9/1.9/(10.6)

Exhibit 2-6: Summary of Financial Statement Measures Used in Stock Market Analysis

General Category	Representative Measures	Flaw
Absolute dollar calculations	Working capital	varying degrees of liquidity
	Cash flow	management's plans for the cash unknown
	Book value	does not include important non-balance sheet assets
Cash budgeting		ignores fluctuations within cycle
Earnings per share (EPS)		"earnings" measurement problems
Discounted cash flow analysis	Amount of future earnings	"earnings" measurement problems
	% of those earnings that will be paid as dividends	dividend policy depends on company's cash requirements and investor expectations
	Applicable discount rate	based on risk-free rate + Beta
Liquidity ratios	Current ratio; quick ratio	only measure the ability of a company to pay its bills
Activity Ratios	Collection period; sales/ inventory	helpful for detail on specific operations, not for investment decisions
Profitability Ratios	Return on sales; return on assets; return on net worth	"earnings" measurement problems

- Or does it indicate that the company has successfully reinvented itself into a 21st century warrior and may be more profitable than its competitors?

- Does a company have sufficient liquidity to pay its bills, or is it aggressively managing cash to nearly zero and using receipts from receivables to meet current needs (supported by a bank line of credit)?

The entire normal range concept is suspect, for who is to say that a company is overusing its working capital or other resources. In fact the very word "normal" implies average, and if we are going to outperform the stock market, why would we want to invest in an average company?

FLAWS IN TRADITIONAL FINANCIAL MEASURES

Exhibit 2-6 summarizes our findings on financial statement information commonly used in stock market analysis. There are more general reasons that ratios and other measures are inadequate.

The Peer Group Comparison Problem

No company can be directly compared with any other company or with any group of companies. There is so much variation in size, geographic market coverage, product line, and distribution system that each company is unique. Certain data services attempt to solve this problem by developing data by asset or sales size, and by aggregating companies into industries and groups within those industries (using U.S. Department of Commerce SIC [Standard Industrial Code] classifications). This is not a fatal flaw in measuring company performance, but should be understood by the investor in developing or using comparative data.

The Mystery of the Undervalued Asset

Other assets do appear on the balance sheet, but due to the conservatism of the accounting profession, are valued at the lower of cost or market. For example, inventory costing $10,000 to produce and marketable for $20,000 is carried on the books at $10,000 until sold. This is probably a fair procedure, because we really don't know until the sale occurs (and the money received) that the inventory is actually worth $20,000.

However, certain other assets really do have a higher value than is shown on the balance sheet. A patent or copyright can be carried as an asset, but only at its development cost if generated internally and at its acquisition cost if purchased. A patent on an innovative discovery costing $10,000 can be worth $1 million, but the balance sheet shows $10,000 (which is then amortized over the life of the patent). When we consider a technology company, such as HWP, we cannot derive much realistic data from the financial statements because of this accounting treatment.

The "Moment in Time" Dilemma

All measures of business activity cut-off at specific times in order to allow the closing of accounting records. The problem with using information as of a moment in time is that various adjustments are often made in "cleaning up" the financial statements to enhance the presentation appearance. Furthermore, businesses subject to seasonal or cyclical change may not be fairly represented at the time the accounting books are closed. Like the peer group comparison problem, this is not a fatal flaw in measuring company performance but should be understood by the investor in considering a stock market purchase.

The Issue of Liquidity versus Growth

While investors may buy earnings growth, they use techniques which largely focus on liquidity or solvency. Most generally accepted measures have been developed to determine if a company can pay its bills or is facing a possible cash shortage. The idea is for creditors to avoid such borrowers and customers, which historically was the basis of many of the criteria we have reviewed. Potential earnings growth is not evaluated very effectively by any of these techniques, and in fact, there really never has been a good measure to assist an investor to do the one thing necessary in stock market investing: forecast whether a company will be profitable in the future.

QUALITATIVE COMMENTARY AND ANALYSIS

Recognizing that strictly quantitative measures do not fully show a company's business or earnings prospects, most of the publishers of financial information attempt to provide business and/or industry summaries. Value Line and Standard & Poor's provide both, and Value Line's late 1996 review of the computer industry[5] and HWP[6] contained the following wisdom:

> "The news from the economic front is generally favorable for the computer industry ... Manufacturers of mainframes ... did not fare particularly well during the first nine months of the year. That was largely a product transition issue, though [as certain companies] are all rolling out new families of mainframes...this industry appears to be well-positioned to post good sales and profit gains for the foreseeable future."

Various factors affecting HWP's sales are noted, including inkjet pricing pressures, disk-drive operational losses, product transitions, slow order growth, hesitancy among software developers to adapt to new processing equipment, and continued domination of the personal computer printer market. Earnings estimates are made for 1997 ($2.90/share) and the year 2000 ($5.00/share).

Standard & Poor's cited the various negatives noted by Value Line, but believed these problems were temporary. They expected that HWP will experience faster growth than the industry over the next several years.[7] A different opinion was offered by Salomon Smith Barney, a large securities firm. While acknowledging HWP as the best managed firm in the industry, various difficulties reduced the likelihood of a significant increase in the price of the stock.[8]

These services focused on product and competitive issues, largely because they could not examine operational issues. In other words, even the most respected analyst cannot climb inside of a company to really learn about critical internal activities and to measure performance except on an aggregated basis. What is presented is certainly interesting and may even be valid. It simply doesn't get at the factors which will eventually drive the stock price.

Conclusions on Traditional Stock Market Measures

As we can see from this discussion of the various traditional stock market measures, HWP's results, like any company's results, are not very useful to the investor in diagnosing specific problems or causes of superior performance. They even may be misleading to a significant extent.

---

[5] Issue of October 25, 1996, p. 1075.

[6] *Ibid.*, p. 1094.

[7] Comment on July 22, 1996.

[8] "The Computer Monitor," November 1996, p. 18

We may have concluded that the various liquidity and activity ratios were sufficiently consistent with the computer industry for the profitability ratios to lead our decision to invest in HWP. If we had made that decision in 1996, we would have seen our per share investment rise from the mid-40s (assuming the average 1996 price) to 80 by 1998 and 150 at the high of the 2000 bull market, a 35% annual return not including a small dividend payout!

However, HWP was selling for about 30 by early 2001, due primarily to the general stock market decline, but also because of the growing perception of the company as stodgy with mature products in a highly competitive technology environment. The need for fresh ideas led to the retirement of the 1995 chairman Lewis Platt; the appointment of Carly Fiorina as the new chairman; new initiatives in PCs, consumer products and Internet services; and a gradual de-emphasis of reliance on printers as the lead product. Interestingly, the ROE remained in the 15% to 20% range during the entire 1993-2000 period we've referenced in this chapter.

HWP experienced a stock price "roller coaster" during these years. The investor should wonder how a consistently high ROE and exemplary results in other quantitative measures can lead to this outcome. Does this perhaps suggest that the information content of the data presented in financial statements is of limited use in selecting stocks for investment?

We conclude that these data *are* misleading and reveal little of predictive value. The analytical procedures used to evaluate financial statement data do nothing to correct or compensate for this problem. Some techniques are either extremely simplistic, providing no analytical content, such as the calculation of the dollars of working capital. Other techniques, such as discounted cash flow, use complex assumptions to hopelessly muddle the analysis.

Chapter 3

Why the Reported Numbers Don't Matter

Annual income twenty pounds, annual expenditure nineteen six, result happiness. Annual income twenty pounds, annual expenditure twenty pounds ought and six, result misery.
Charles Dickens, *1812-1870 (David Copperfield, ch. 12)*

The three basic stock market investment theories discussed in Chapter 1 have an appealing — but misleading — common attribute: a heavy reliance on numbers. Each theory quantifies company, market or general economic data to justify a stock selection. Quantitative analysis provides the appearance of precision and objectivity, a "scientific" methodology applied to a very human and subjective field of investigation. This chapter examines numerical measures of company performance as guidance to the prediction of stock market results, and analyzes their flaws.

EARNINGS AS THE DRIVER OF STOCK PRICES

Except for technical analysts, the common wisdom is that earnings (or net income) drives the price of a stock. Investors buy current and future profits, often measured as earnings per share (EPS). EPS are compared to the market price of a stock through the price-earnings ratio (P/E). This ratio presumably shows whether the price of a stock is a "fair" price. It is derived from projected EPS times a multiplier (the P/E) based on required earnings for companies in that same industry with similar characteristics.

In buying earnings, investors are faced with investments exhibiting various levels of risk. We discussed one generally accepted approach to measuring risk and returns in Chapter 1, in our discussion of the efficient market theory and Beta. One component of the efficient market theory is to compare alternative returns on invested capital or common equity (ROE) among investments with equivalent risk profiles. We could compare equivalent size companies in an industry, with a preference for the business reporting the highest ROE (and hopefully a "reasonable" P/E).

A simple example would be in paper and forest products, as shown in Exhibit 3-1. We might jump at Fort James, with its 31% ROE and reasonable P/E of 12 times. This approach seems logical until we examine similar statistics (in Exhibit 3-2) for all 24 industry groups reported by *Business Week*.

Exhibit 3-1: Paper and Forest Products Company P/Es and ROEs

	P/E Ratio	ROE
Georgia-Pacific	9	20.1%
Kimberly-Clark	17	32.5%
Weyerhauser	17	12.9%
Champion International	15	12.2%
Williamette Industries	21	7.7%
Louisiana-Pacific	6	15.9%
Boise Cascade	10	12.1%
Mead	15	8.6%
Fort James	12	31.0%
International Paper	77	1.6%
Potlatch	27	4.4%
All Companies	15	12.3%

Source: *Business Week* Annual Issue, March 27, 2000, pp. 167-193.

Exhibit 3-2: Industry Sector P/Es and ROEs
(arrayed in descending P/E Ratio order)

	P/E Ratio	ROE %
Telecommunications	62	12.2
Electrical and Electronics	54	14.3
Metals and Mining	47	5.9
Office Equipment and Computers	47	21.4
Service Industries	37	7.6
Healthcare (including Pharmaceuticals)	29	25.2
Conglomerates	26	23.9
Fuel	24	13.4
Publishing and Broadcasting	22	15.0
Chemicals	21	10.1
Consumer Products	21	26.5
Food	21	23.6
Leisure Time Industries	20	11.7
Discount and Fashion Retailing	19	17.8
Manufacturing	18	14.5
Containers and Packaging	16	9.5
Paper and Forest Products	15	12.3
Nonbank Financial	14	17.3
Banks	13	18.7
Utilities	13	11.1
Aerospace and Defense	12	13.3
Transportation	11	11.5
Housing and Real Estate	8	22.2
Automotive	7	25.6
All-Industry Composite (unweighted)	24	16.0

Source: *Business Week* Annual Issue, March 27, 2000, pp. 167-193.

The reported P/Es range from 7 to 62. However, the corresponding ROEs do not appear to correlate with the P/Es; some low P/E industries have high ROEs, while some high P/E industries have low ROEs. It is clear that investors are not very trusting or do not feel terribly confident in some component of either the P/E or the ROE, or both. These results show the inherent weakness in using earnings to project fair stock market prices.

The common wisdom is that companies manifesting strength, growth, and proven success will sell at a high P/E multiple, except in cases of temporarily depressed earnings or in situations where an emerging company is operating at or near a loss. The problem of P/Es is not in the numerator of that ratio, as the market price of a stock is *the* price, and by definition, is correct. The problem is with the denominator, the definition of earnings, and the problem with how earnings are calculated so pervades stock market analysis that it makes such efforts effectively worthless. Let us see why.

Interpreting Accrual Accounting Results

Generally accepted accounting principles ("GAAP") allow considerable leeway in the statement of business income. "Accrual accounting" assigns costs to the timing of the sale of product rather than to the time that the cost was incurred, and recognizes sales at the time of invoicing rather than at the time that funds are received. ("Cash accounting," which recognizes sales and costs at the time when cash is received or spent, is used primarily by small businesses.)

Both the nature of accrual accounting and the permitted leeway in the interpretation of the recording of business events allow companies to report earnings which may not accurately reflect economic results. This is not a revolutionary idea; in fact, the outstanding source on the difficulties in using accounting income for stock market analysis is Benjamin Graham and David Dodd's *Security Analysis*, originally published in 1934.[1]

The authors devote nearly one-fourth of their text to the necessary adjustments to reported earnings for fundamental stock analysis. They suggest seven steps to properly re-compute earnings, as listed in Exhibit 3-3. Each financial statement element must be examined for any unrepresentative revenue or expense that interferes with the presentation of continuing operations.

These adjustments are developed in some detail to support the accurate determination of earnings. However, there is considerable judgment involved in this work, potentially distorting company results far more than the numbers reported on the income statement. Furthermore, the pressure on company management today to meet or beat stock analysts' quarterly earnings estimates is so great, and the markets react so harshly when such estimates fall short, that any earnings must be treated with suspicion.

---

[1] See the 5th edition by Sidney Cottle *et. al.*, McGraw-Hill, 1988.

Exhibit 3-3: Graham and Dodd Earnings Restatement Procedures

1. *Restate non-recurring income or expenses*, such as litigation costs, tax adjustments, asset sales, the write-up or write-down of investments, the gains or losses from foreign exchange, and the costs of discontinued operations. These costs are particularly important in this period of downsizing and restructuring.

2. *Eliminate any unjustified recognition of income.* Graham and Dodd cite manager compensation by stock options as an example of a cost which is not recognized by the rules of accounting. Any off-balance sheet item would be suspect as having an effect on economic income, such as a company's obligation for lease payments. Outsourcing has significantly increased the potential for earnings distortion through the use of such devices.

3. *Correct any direct entries to net worth*, such as reserve accounts for possible future contingencies. A "reserve account" is a segregation of an amount from retained earnings for a possible future contingent event, so that those funds will not be spent on dividends or investment in the development of the business. Graham and Dodd list the primary types of reserves as valuation accounts, such as for uncollectible receivables; liabilities, such as for taxes or for litigation claims; and future development reserves, such as for business restructuring.

4. *Analyze methods of inventory costing and depreciation.* Inventory costing is most often a choice between FIFO (first in, first out) and LIFO (last in, last out) evaluation methods. The usual practice in a business is to sell the oldest inventory, so that remaining stock will be "fresh." However, LIFO costing assumes that the most recent inventory has been sold, as newer inventory is likely to be more costly (in an inflationary environment). The earnings (and income taxes) that result from the sale are reduced to compensate the business for the impact of inflation.

    Similarly, depreciation can be assigned to an asset on an accelerated basis (such as "sum-of-the-years-digits") rather than straight-line (an equal amount each year of the asset's life), to accomplish a reduction in reported income in the first years of an asset's life.

5. *Adjust earnings resulting from the operations of subsidiaries and affiliates.* This would include joint ventures, investments carried at their cost, foreign operations, and certain other activities.

6. *Recalculate income taxes, based on the preceding adjustments.* The complexity of corporate taxes makes it impossible to provide a comprehensive listing of such changes. However, selected changes include bracket jump due to the progressive structure of the tax code; the alternative minimum tax which requires that at least some taxes be paid regardless of accounting profits if tax preferences are claimed; effects of tax credits for certain activities encouraged by the tax code; and the effect of the carry forward or carry back of operating losses (where losses are used to offset profits in previous or future years to reduce taxes).

7. *Include/exclude certain unrecorded assets and liabilities*, such as pension fund assets, cash balances required to support credit lines as required by bank lending agreements, inadequate loss reserves from doubtful accounts receivable ("bad debts"), unsalable inventory, the market value of appreciated fixed assets, and appropriate alterations to various other accounts.

Source: Benjamin Graham and David Dodd, *Security Analysis* (5th edition by Sidney Cottle *et. al.*, McGraw-Hill, 1988), Chapters 10-20.

"Managed" Earnings

The Securities and Exchange Commission is deeply concerned about the management of reported EPS to satisfy Wall Street's demands.[2] Accounting "tricks" to manage earnings include a variety of revenue enhancement and expense recognition or deferral actions.[3]

- Significant differences between earnings and cash flow. We defined "cash flow" in Chapter 2 as "EBITDA," or earnings before interest, taxes, depreciation, and amortization. A large variance could mean an attempt to manage the recognition of revenues or costs.

- Balance sheet disparities in earnings reported to shareholders and the Internal Revenue Service. Companies maintaining two sets of accounting books are required to indicate significant variations in their financial statement footnotes.

- Unsustainable sales results. These may result from unusual marketing activities such as pricing below cost to clear inventory.

- The overuse of reserves to smooth future earnings. "Reserves" are set-asides of earnings for future contingencies, and are appropriate for such uses as the settlement of legal actions but not to manage earnings.

- The deferral of expenses, indicating that costs are not being matched against revenues in the period incurred. Such deferrals are carried as an asset and are amortized over time, but should usually be expensed in the current period.

- Reductions of core activities to enhance current period earnings. Such expenses as technology-related research and development are essential for the future of the business, but may be cut to manage reported results.

- The overstatement of gross margins and relative ratios by labeling certain expenses as marketing costs rather than as costs of goods sold. This has been a particular problem in Internet retail selling.[4]

GAAP requires accounting charges against earnings for non-recurring losses, which are assumed to be one-time events by investors and analysts. A review of GAAP recurring charges of such companies as Intel, AT&T, and Westinghouse shows that there is a trend to write-off ongoing expenses to inflate future

---

[2] See Carol J. Loomis, "Lies, Damned Lies, and Managed Earnings," *Fortune Magazine*, August 2, 1999, pp. 74-92.

[3] For a review of these tricks, see Gretchen Morgenson, "When a Rosy Picture Should Raise a Red Flag," *The New York Times*, July 18, 1999, §III, p. 6.

[4] This problem was reported by Elizabeth Macdonald, "Fess-Up Time," *Forbes Magazine*, September 18, 2000, pp. 80-84.

earnings. Restructuring charges in large publicly traded companies had become a common occurrence during the 1990s. For example, IBM's restructuring charges were $6.3 billion *more* than reported profits in the 1991-1995 period.[5]

Given these actions by management to manage earnings, it is difficult to specify what "true" earnings are. As the result, attempts at evaluating a company by analyzing earnings are a waste of time. With all due respect to Graham and Dodd or other fundamental stock market gurus, it simply can't be done with any degree of accuracy due to the large number of possible changes and the extent of judgment required.

FRAUD IN EARNINGS RESULTS

The investing public is somewhat protected by independent audits of accounting records and by opinions as to the accuracy of the financial statements. However, the accountant's objective has never been to probe into and report fraudulent practices or to provide notice of any possible problems.

Carefully written opinions are prepared concerning the scope of the audit. Typical language: "These financial statements are the responsibility of the company's management. Our responsibility is to express an opinion on the statements based on our audits." A shrewdly engineered fraud will not likely be discovered in an examination given current practice and the accounting profession's difficulty in attracting new and in retaining experienced auditors.[6] The discovery of a fraud does not compel public disclosure, although the auditing firm typically withdraws from the client.

Reports of Fraud

The rise in fraud has been subject to scathing SEC and U.S. Department of Justice criticism and, in the more egregious cases, by criminal prosecution. In addition to the situations noted below, *Fortune Magazine* has compiled a list of ten corporate situations resulting in jail terms of up to 20 years for various types of criminal fraud.[7]

Some examples of frauds in the last decade include:

- On January 29, 1997, Mercury Finance announced that earnings would be restated for four (!) years, causing the stock price to drop 86%. Some important analysts were fooled by Mercury's story prior to the earnings surprise, including *Forbes Magazine* and *Barron's* which published positive reviews of the company.[8]

---

[5] See Frank Lalli, "The Real Dow," *Money Magazine*, March 1997, pp. 76-79.

[6] See Melody Petersen, "Shortage of Accounting Students Raises Concern on Audit Quality," *The New York Times*, February 19, 1999, pp. A1, C3.

[7] Loomis, *op cit.*, p. 6. For other situations of financial statement fraud, see Howard M. Schilit, *Financial Shennanigans: How to Detect Accounting Gimmicks & Fraud in Financial Reports,* McGraw-Hill, 1993.

[8] W. Stern, "Investigate Your Customer," *Forbes*, September 13, 1993, pp. 171-172, and Andrew Bary, "Steep Incline," *Barron's*, August 15, 1994, pp. 17-18.

- Fraud at apparel maker Leslie Fay Companies in the early 1990s through inventory and sales misstatement was so pervasive that more than two dozen company managers participated. Revenues were stated at budgeted rather than actual levels and involved sales on merchandise shipped to company sites. Stock tags were forged, inventory values were altered, and customers were charged less than production costs to boost sales.

- Incidents of fraudulent financial statements include California Micro Devices, which announced inflated and nonexistent sales; Kidder Peabody (owned by General Electric), which experienced a systematic fraud by trader Joseph Jett of $350 million; and numerous savings and loan and thrift industry frauds.

- Accounting irregularities were reported at Nine West, which had been under SEC investigation for how revenues were recognized following their 1995 acquisition of U.S. Shoe.

- Livent, the theatrical producer of such shows as "Show Boat" and "Ragtime," has been accused by the SEC of masking losses, shifting costs between productions, and cooking their books to raise nearly $200 million in debt and equity capital.

THE ROLE OF THE ACCOUNTANT

Investors have been challenging the notion of the auditor as a detached agent who is free of responsibility for developments proceeding the audit. These challenges, in the form of high-priced litigation claims, have posed a mounting threat to public accountancy. As the result of numerous instances of financial statement fraud, a new profession has appeared: the fraud or forensic accountant.[9]

Many observers feel that this threat has developed into a crisis unlike any the profession has ever encountered. Beginning in 1990, accountants began to face an ever-increasing tidal wave of litigation suits put forth for the most part by plaintiffs who had lost large sums of money in failed savings and loans. These investors felt that auditors were to blame for not uncovering and disclosing the rampant fraud that was characteristic of many of the failures within the thrift industry.

As evidenced by their lawsuits, investors seem to expect auditors' opinions to provide a "seal of approval" and an assurance of fraud disclosure. Are these expectations reasonable? An argument can be made that if auditors had been more vocal in the S&L situation, or in other recent cases, billions of taxpayer, investor and creditor dollars and thousands of jobs would have been saved. Instead, their $50 billion in accounting fee revenue may have been the compelling interest, rather than disclosure.

---

[9] See, for example, G. Jack Bologna and Robert J. Lindquist, *Fraud Auditing and Forensic Accounting: New Tools and Techniques, 2nd edition*, John Wiley & Sons, 1995.

Some degree of further auditor independence will be achieved by the adoption of a SEC rule in late 2000 limiting consulting work for audit clients. The new rule requires that audit committees of corporate boards review whether non-audit services are consistent with auditor independence. While this step should reduce the inevitable conflict of interest when audits and consulting are performed by the same firm, other problems remain.

Auditor Limitations

There currently exist general ambiguity and lack of consensus as to what precisely is the role of the auditor. In conducting audits, accountants follow generally accepted auditing standards to obtain *reasonable assurance* about whether the financial statements are free of *material misstatement* (from typical opinion language). What do the terms in italics mean? The language of the opinion is certainly ambiguous and subject to misinterpretation.

Investors should not assume that fraud is pervasive in publicly held companies. However, financial reporting is subject to the limitations of auditor review and senior management honesty. In an environment of ever increasing demands on reported financial results, earnings may not be as reliable as we might wish.

Although measures of earnings are ambiguous, the reality is that reported earnings, as interpreted by investors, drive stock prices. In many ways this explains the concept of an auction market, with buyers of stocks anticipating higher earnings, based on their interpretation of business information, and sellers anticipating lower or flat earnings based on that same data.

ASSETS THAT CAN'T BE MEASURED

As we begin the 21st century, business is evolving from a fixed asset orientation (as in a traditional manufacturing company) to a focus on cash, people and knowledge (as in a high tech company). Financial reporting has always been based on the issues of legal ownership and debt. A business must have the right to control or use a resource, or must owe a debt, for an entry to appear on the balance sheet. Without ownership or control, there cannot be a claim of value for that resource.

How We Account For People

People are now the most important resource in a business, yet are neither owned nor controlled by their organizations. Humans can walk in or out of the employment door at any time, and employers enjoy "employment at will" status in most states, the right to hire and fire without cause (except for protected classes under equal employment opportunity regulations).

These guarantees preclude accountants from recognizing the value of employees in financial reports, except for the reporting of salary and benefits costs on the income statement. The group of employees who develop and market computer chips, though of inestimable value to a high tech computer company, would be carried on the balance sheet as having zero value.

Measures of or surrogates for these missing assets have been suggested at various times, but have never received widespread acceptance. For example, salary surveys are published annually by *Business Week*, but these data only apply to a few senior managers. A reasonable attempt is made by that publication to determine the effectiveness of these managers as compared to company profitability and stock price performance. However, the data do not reach down into the managers, sales staff, and technicians who bring value added to their organizations through their marketing, financial, production or engineering skills.

Other Missing Assets

Other critical non-balance sheet assets reflect progress in marketing, including customer loyalty, product development, marketplace acceptance, and innovation; the development of proprietary systems capabilities; and labor and manager peace and cooperation. These assets impact each other in a dynamic, synergistic way, and can provide a combined result considerably more than the value of the individual components.[10]

Due to the inherent conservatism of accounting, knowledge about product innovation or discoveries is carried on financial statements at the cost of development or acquisition. Included in the development costs are experiments, the construction of working models, and the patent application procedure (including drawings, attorney's fees, and filing expenses). No estimation is attempted for the market value of the resulting patent, copyright or new product, either as to a price in a sale or the earnings power of the discovery over the effective life. A computer chip costing $5 million to develop but with a fair market value of $500 million would be carried at $5 million.

The Fallacy of Numbers

In this environment, traditional financial measures are useless in business analysis and investment decisions. We calculate values for current and fixed assets, yet working capital and most fixed assets are drags on financial performance and are therefore undesirable. We place little or no value on people and new technology, yet these are the most valuable resources (along with cash) that most companies have. Financial statements have a Newtonian view of the world: they attempt to precisely measure physical assets and the debts incurred in acquiring those assets. In effect, we count the things that increasingly don't matter and ignore the things that inevitably do matter.

That's not to say that this situation is ignored by the business press or by companies. *Fortune* discussed the importance of *intellectual capital* to U.S. companies, emphasizing specific instances of scientific discovery and innovation.[11] *Plan-*

---

[10] For a discussion of efforts at developing measures of performance in these areas, see Michael Baltes, "Measuring Non-Financial Assets," *Wharton Magazine*, Winter 1997, pp. 7-12.

[11] "Brainpower," June 3, 1991, pp. 44-60.

ning Review used a different phrase but made the same points.[12] One writer suggests that the idea of control of the human resource is solved by considering employees as owners rather than assets, through the vigorous use of programs to enable stock ownership (such as stock options, bonuses paid partially in stock, and similar devices).[13]

Nearly every annual report acknowledges the contribution of employees to the past year's results. Hewlett-Packard noted that its strong 1995 results were accomplished with a small increase in headcount. "That's a real tribute to HP's (HWP) people, who continued to show tremendous skill, energy and resourcefulness in anticipating and responding to customer needs."[14] But nowhere do HWP's people appear in the financial statements!

The Stock Market Isn't Fooled

The economic importance of human resources to new economy businesses is unmistakable,[15] and the importance of people to business can be seen in Exhibit 3-2 where we arrayed *Business Week's* industry groups in descending price-earnings (P-E) ratio order. Industries with high market P/E ratios are those with creative or scientific products and services, such as telecommunications, electronics, office equipment and computers, healthcare and pharmaceuticals, and publishing and broadcasting. Industries with lower valuations are oriented to more repetitive processes, including containers and packaging, paper and forest products, transportation and utilities.

FINANCIAL STATEMENT LEVERAGE

The new emphasis in business is on reducing current and fixed asset accounts and funding current liabilities entirely from the ongoing operations of the business. A company's balance sheet contributes directly to its income statement through the allocation of assets to support the various operational activities of a company. The impact of this interrelationship is referred to as "leverage." Let's examine this impact on earnings and financing decisions.

Cash collected from sales is used for payables and payroll, with only a minimum amount left idle in the current assets account. The result is the use of leverage to generate higher sales and earnings by trading on the company's market presence. In other words, retaining minimal non-productive assets on the balance sheet is feasible if the company is credible to its suppliers, banks, and other constituents.

---

[12] Kathryn R. Harrigan and Gaurav Dalmia, "Knowledge Workers: The Last Bastion of Competitive Advantage," *Planning Review*, November-December 1991, pp. 4-9, 48.

[13] Thomas A. Stewart, *Intellectual Capital*, Doubleday/Currency, 1997.

[14] Chairman's letter, p. 2, *1995 Annual Report*.

[15] There is a growing body of work on human or intellectual capital. See, for example, Thomas O. Davenport, *Human Capital: What It Is and Why People Invest It*, Jossey-Bass Publishers, 1999. A recent article discusses the business of licensing such intellectual assets as patents, copyrights and business practices; Carol O. Madigan, "Capitalizing on Intellectual Capital," *Business Finance*, May 2000, pp. 79-86.

Earnings Leverage

The balance sheet contributes directly to the income statement by the allocation of assets to support various operational activities. For example, if a company invests in low growth activities rather than outsourcing the function those assets support, the earnings generated by the balance sheet will likely be less than could potentially have been earned from essential or high growth activities.

A careful examination of balance sheet accounts may show that a smaller holding of certain assets would be feasible, and scarce resources would then be freed for other uses. Such other uses could include investing in short-term assets to improve the working capital position, acquiring productive assets and investments, paying down liabilities, and/or distribution to shareholders as dividends. These are management decisions which are difficult to directly observe from published company financial or business data.

Access to internal company records would allow us to examine each process to determine which assets support core business activities and should be retained. At the same time, we could ascertain which assets are used for non-essential activities and could be reassigned. The problem is that we cannot directly measure earnings leverage. We do not have access to the accounting ledgers of the company to determine which assets support core activities and which support non-essential activities. Executive and managers of the company have access to his information, and are best able to make business decisions on the deployment of scarce company resources.

Financing Leverage

The balance sheet also contributes to the income statement by the financing of enterprise business activities. This may be considered as "financing leverage." The financing of assets is accomplished through either debt or equity, each of which incurs a cost (known as the cost of debt capital and the cost of equity capital).

In capital budgeting, any project with a higher internal rate of return (IRR) than the correspondent cost of capital can be considered as a potential investment. A decision to invest will contribute to earnings whenever the IRR is greater or equal to the cost of capital. In fact, two things occur as scarce capital is used:

 • The cost of future financings rise.

 • It may be necessary to postpone or cancel activities with potentially higher returns.

These two phenomenon are well established in corporate finance.

We cannot directly measure financing leverage because we do not have access to financial market intelligence on the company's cost of capital under different financing scenarios. We can estimate a company's cost to raise debt or equity capital, based on general market conditions. However, the precise content of this data, like earning leverage information, is accessible only to company managers and their advisors, who make decisions on raising and using capital.

The Investor's Dilemma

We simply cannot see into the minds and hearts of a group of managers and their advisors to determine whether their decisions are in the best long-term interests of investors. As investors, we must face the dilemma that we cannot gain access to the very data which would assist us in evaluating potential investments. It can be seen that the essential elements of company evaluation are hidden from public observation. In a sense, the company is a "black box" in its development and analysis of data and its use of those data in its decision-making.

Fundamental analysis assumes that available economic and business data tell us all that we need to know about a company and its industry, with particular focus on restated earnings (per Graham and Dodd) as measured against invested capital (ROE). To summarize our assumptions:

- Reported earnings are estimations of the past reporting period and cannot be properly restated.

- We cannot directly know the important developments in a company.

- The best that we can do is to indirectly analyze performance through the evaluation of various income statement and balance sheet data.

Despite the torrent of financial and business data available to investors, there is insufficient public information on asset use, costs of capital and financing alternatives, and the correct calculation of earnings. The problem of being able to do insightful fundamental analysis is further complicated by management's decisions on paying dividends or retaining earnings to invest in future internal growth.

There is quite a theoretical literature on dividend policy in finance journals, the general tone of which follows the work of Franco Modigliani and Merton Miller (MM).[16] MM maintain that dividend policy is irrelevant (even for investors desiring a present-day cash return). If there is an insufficient dividend payout, shareholders are free to sell stock on the open market. However, the investor simply cannot know what the correct decision is — to pay dividends or to reinvest earnings in the company — and *must* rely on management to attempt to construct a net worth for the company which best supports future business activities.

The traditional measures of company performance do not provide much guidance to the prediction of stock market results. Despite the title of this chapter ("Why the Reported Numbers Don't Matter"), we now know that financial information does matter — it's just that we cannot measure it accurately.

---

[16] "Dividend Policy, Growth and the Valuation of Shares," *Journal of Business*, October 1961, pp. 411-433.

Chapter 4

The Enigma of the Business Enterprise

It is a riddle wrapped in a mystery inside an enigma.
Winston Churchill, *1874-1965 (referring to the Soviet Union)*

Chapters 2 and 3 discussed traditional, quantitative methodologies for analyzing the performance of a business enterprise. We have seen that accounting and financial data are historical, somewhat misleading and largely useless as indicators of a company's future stock price. This chapter discusses the blackbox that is the modern corporation, one so impervious to understanding that investors, stock analysts, and even management cannot make rational sense out of what's going on!

THE "SCIENCE" OF BUSINESS

Attempts to develop principles of business are the natural outcome of hundreds of years of inquiry into laws of physical and social sciences. This investigation can be traced as far back as Isaac Newton's *Principia* (1687), which described the three basic laws of motion — inertia, acceleration and action, and reaction; the two laws of conservation — conservation of mass and conservation of momentum; and the law of gravitation.

Early social scientists who followed Newton in a search for laws of human and organizational behavior included Adam Smith, the father of economics, and Auguste Comte, the father of sociology. The idea that simple, logical laws determine the behavior of workers and businesses is extremely appealing, and given the vast complexity of large corporations, it would greatly simplify the analytical work necessary to evaluate a potential stock market investment.

As modern physicists have shown in the theory of relativity and in quantum mechanics, it is impossible under certain conditions to precisely determine the behavior of selected physical elements. It has become equally apparent in the social sciences that the measurement of results using simplistic yardsticks is a futile exercise. We may be attracted to a set of numerical metrics to forecast stock performance, but that does not necessary make such measures valid.

The Levels of Management

The modern corporation has six or more reporting levels from the chief executive officer (CEO) to the lowest level supervisor. This arrangement developed historically to ease the span of control burden on each manager, the number of reporting relationships that each superior manager would have with his or her subordinates.

Consider the CEO as Management Level 1, his or her direct reports, such as Executive Vice Presidents and the Chief Financial Officer as Management Level 2, and their direct reports, such as Marketing and Manufacturing Vice Presidents and the Treasurer as Management Level 3. By the time you get to the layer where the real work is done, say Management Level 6 (the SBU or strategic business unit managers), it is impossible for the Management Level 1 manager to understand what the Management Level 6 manager does all day.

Decision-Making Responsibilities

Our experience is that there are three types of managerial decisions which impact earnings.

- Strategic decisions involve grand issues affecting the future direction of the company, including the acquisition or sale of business units, new products or services offered, markets served, and the financing of these activities. These decisions are typically made at Management Levels 1 and 2.

- Operating decisions involve sales and marketing, pricing, features offered, customer service, and similar considerations in support of the work of the SBU. Many large companies are organized around SBUs for the sake of convenience, so that accountability for the use of resources can reside within a defined organizational element of appropriate size. Operating decisions are typically made at Management Levels 3 and 4.

- Activity decisions involve the day-to-day functioning of the company at the supervisor or first level manager level, and include such issues as the priority for the assignment of work and its sequencing; arranging for workers, equipment and raw materials; and dealing with customer demands and problems. These decisions are typically made at Management Levels 5 and 6.

All three levels of decisions obviously impact the company's success. However, operating decisions — those at Levels 3 and 4 — probably most directly impact earnings results. It is at these levels where customers are gained or lost through sales efforts, where innovation and research is approved or denied, where workers are attracted and kept or repelled, and where production process quality is maintained or destroyed. These efforts are critical to a business, yet Level 1 and 2 managers seldom get involved in these activities except when an important customer comes to town or when a major decision is about to be made.

Internal Expansion versus Merger and Acquisition

A generation or so ago businesses grew from within, by expanding a basic idea into a vertically and/or horizontally integrated organization.

- "Horizon integration" involves expanding into new markets at the same level of distribution, as when a food store becomes a supermarket.

- "Vertical integration" expands earlier or later in the channel of distribution, as in the situation where an automobile manufacturer expands backward to own steel mills or forward to own an automobile financing facility.

The entrepreneurs who led those businesses often had intimate knowledge of their organizations; outstanding examples are Henry Ford of Ford Motor and Sam Walton of Wal-Mart.

Companies in the present generation often grow by combination rather than internal growth, buying proven success in competitive or complementary businesses. Merger and acquisition activity was about $3.5 trillion in the U.S. and Europe in 1999, about ten times the level in the early 1990s. This trend will undoubtedly continue as globalization eliminates smaller competitors.

The acquisition of production processes, market share, distribution, and financing is frequently more efficient than attempting to build these functions. However, the opportunity to know the employees, manufacturing facilities, vendors, systems and customers is lost, and senior executives must depend on reporting through corporate intelligence systems.

Corporate Intelligence

Much of the data available to Level 1 and 2 managers are oriented to counting transactions, rather than to thoughtful analysis. *Business Week* reports that companies which have systems providing corporate intelligence are the exception, representing perhaps no more than 15% of all large companies.[1] The other four-fifths plus of such companies are restricted to the data provided by such traditional systems as accounts payable and receivable, the general ledger, sales activity reporting, and payroll.

While this may seem appropriate support for the manager's job, the problem is that counting transactions is not terribly useful in developing a framework for strategic or operational decision-making. As the result, senior managers (Levels 1 and 2) spend much of their time reviewing activity summaries, distilled from various reports prepared by Level 3 and 4 managers. And those summaries often contain the most favorable news, not the lost customers, the production problems or comments on the low morale of the workers.

---

[1] "Beyond Bean-Counting," October 28, 1996, p. 131. However, this statistic has been increasing in the past few years due to the installation of enterprise resource systems (ERPs).

21st Century Business Leadership

Level 1 and 2 managers seldom interact with Levels 3 and 4, and almost never with Levels 5 and 6. Often they know that a transaction occurred, but none of the details, sweat, cost, and lost opportunity of that transaction. In other words, a common state of things is for the senior managers of a large corporation to not really understand or want to find out what is going on inside of their own companies.

Here are two examples of senior management behavior from our consulting experience.

- The chairman of a multi-billion financial services organization managed some 200 SBUs in the U.S. and 25 international locations. Although he had an idea what was going on in these businesses, it was physically impossible for him to know the details of each activity or the promises made to each client by the various salespeople. Management was by summary report, distilled from yet other reports, all of which were based on budget targets set by a planning group.

    The budget had to be met to make profit numbers promised to stock analysts, shareholders, and the board of directors. However, budget goals had little relationship to realistic targets set by the activity and operating managers who actually had client contact and knew what the competition was doing. As the result, the goals set by senior management were frequently missed, earnings were continuously below expectations, and several of the lower level managers were dismissed. Eventually the board revolted and dismissed the chairman, but not before the company had suffered years of mediocre performance.

- A billion dollar industrial corporation, with locations throughout the U.S., Europe and the Far East, was managed by a CEO with a planning and finance background. He had little production and marketing experience, knew few of the company's customers, and never entered the shop floors, the company's distribution centers or the non-U.S. locations. All such activities were run by the Level 2 managers, who were constantly reporting on how the business was improving.

    The only problem was that things were actually deteriorating, with many sales at a loss, and because of significant quality problems, important business relationships were won by competitors. When these factors were presented to the CEO, he reacted by removing certain key managers but retaining others who were at fault for several of the company's difficulties. Like our financial services company, the board finally got tired of excuses and promises, and removed the CEO.

RECENT MANAGEMENT INNOVATIONS

Various quantitative procedures have been utilized by companies to attempt to control the actions of their Level 3 through 6 managers and business units.

Management-by-Objectives

Management-by-objectives (MBOs) requires the quantification of the manager's objectives as a way of measuring job performance, and then the tracking of performance against those MBOs. For example, an MBO might be to complete all work on customer requests within two days, or to go on 20 marketing trips a year, or to process 100 orders a week. However, MBOs cannot substitute for senior management direction of the efforts of Level 3 through 6 managers for various reasons.

- *Appropriateness of the MBOs.* The accomplishment of the MBOs becomes its own objective or purpose, regardless of the relevance of the MBOs to business conditions changes or reassigned priorities. MBOs are often set for the coming year during the manager's annual review, yet dynamic marketplace and competitive factors may require different responses than were anticipated.

- *Quality or Quantity?* The MBO is a quantifiable metric, but there is no calculation of performance quality. For example, a marketing trip can involve superficial customer visits, lasting 15 minutes long, without any substance and merely intended to help reach the MBO. Or, it can be thoughtfully organized and executed, using a discussion plan, sales brochures, and telephone follow-up. Yet these visits would be equally considered.

- *Relevance of MBOs.* Who is sufficiently perceptive to know if a group of MBOs provides appropriate goals for a manager, or if other, perhaps less quantifiable objectives are better goals? The job of managing workers does not lend itself to a counting standard, because coaching, advising, and teaching cannot be directly measured. The result can be quantified — increased profits, higher worker satisfaction, and fewer accidents or errors — yet these outcomes are difficult to relate back to a manager's performance.

- *Alterations in Business Priorities.* During the year, management's allocation of resources may change due to revisions in the strategies of the business. Many employees are instructed to work on projects for which there is no MBO criterion in their plan, when they had been working industriously toward fulfillment of their MBOs. What happens at the end of the year when there has been progress on the new project but the MBO goal is not met?

The business world often prefers simplicity — counting things — rather than complexity — evaluating the contribution of the manager's performance to company results. It's easier to count units than to do a comprehensive review of a person's value. Counting MBOs may deceive senior management into believing that it understands what's going on in the company, but trusting in numerical objectives doesn't make those MBOs accurate.

Benchmarking

Benchmarking is another technique of control used by companies to focus on the performance of business units. Equivalent tasks are contrasted within and across organizations to specify "best practices." However, many managers do not operate in an environment of standardized outputs, and there can be significant variations in the extent of product development and activities by organizational structure.

The search for a set of "best practices" may be more harmful than beneficial in the determination of acceptable performance, as the focus shifts to a measure of production from the quality of the items produced. For example, once an account payable is authorized, it is unlikely to be subject to further review to determine appropriateness. But there are numerous reviews of that payable which should be performed before a check is written, including:

- accounting codes accuracy

- verification of authorizing signature(s)

- disbursement system coding

- holding disbursement to designated release date

- determination of method of disbursement

These reviews are designed to protect a business's assets, and any acceleration influenced by benchmarks may turn the operation into a production line.

How HWP Handles the Problem

HWP is one of these decentralized, "boundaryless" companies, dedicated to not being a traditional line and staff organization with specified functional borders. This decentralization was in response to an unresponsive centralized organizational focus in the late 1980s, which caused product delays, missed targets, and slowed earnings. HWP essentially is an assembly of separate businesses, not a single organization with Level 1 and 2 managers making decisions. "If any part of the company grows complacent, another part of HWP may eat its lunch..." in fostering internal competition.[2]

---

[2] John H. Sheridan, "Lew Platt: Creating a Culture for Innovation," *Industry Week*, December 19, 1994, pp. 26-30 at p. 28.

The previous CEO Lewis Platt contended that "...senior managements's role is *not* to tell business units what opportunity to take. Instead our role is to create the environment that encourages business managers to take risks and create new growth opportunities."[3] Management is accomplished through a focus on people skills, team building, and positive motivation, not by involving executives in business unit decision-making or operations. Sounds great... but how much can senior managers actually know about the action down in the Level 5 and 6 trenches?

STRATEGIC DECISION-MAKING

Because senior managers don't know what's going on in their own companies, they frequently resort to strategic planning support from their own staff or from consultants. This is a big business involving its own "buzzwords;" some in current or recent use include:

- *coevolution or business ecosystem:* the concept of strategic alliances with customers, suppliers, and even competitors

- *co-opetition:* cooperation and competition between companies in different business areas

- *value migration:* the movement of business opportunities among competitors

- *strategic intent:* a "stretch" business goal or destiny

- *white-space opportunities:* areas of growth which fall between the responsibilities of established organizational units because there is no skill or responsibility match.

Does Planning Work?

Reports of CEOs relying on outside experts include the following cases.[4]

- Sears, Roebuck used a consultant's value migration process to determine that its 15 year decline was because Sears didn't understand its customers. The result was the disposal of non-core assets (such as insurance and stock brokerage services), an upgrading of store appearance, a new emphasis on women's apparel, and a new advertising campaign.

- EDS (Electronic Data Systems) implemented another consultant's strategic intent process to expand its core business, information technology, to serve other client needs and create more comprehensive solutions. One outcome was the purchase of a large management consulting practice, A.T. Kearney.

---

[3] *Ibid.,* p. 26.

[4] These situations are described in "Strategic Planning," *Business Week,* August 26, 1996, pp. 46-52.

- J.M. Smucker, a specialized food company, applied the business ecosystem process to create alliances with other food producers. One example is a venture with confectioners Brach and Brock to make and co-brand jelly-beans and other products.

These theories are making a new generation of consultants wealthy. You may remember that these are the same folks who brought you cows, dogs, stars and question marks in considering alternative strategic plans. "Cows" were boring cash generators, as in "cash cows." "Dogs" were businesses without exciting future prospects. "Stars" were the sexy, likely future winners. "Question marks" were so difficult to categorize that even highly paid consultants couldn't figure them out!

Why Planning Fails

Creativity and the "a ha" moment of insight tend to suffer precisely because strategic planning uses a businesses' existing resource formulation or thought process. What has worked, *e.g.*, cash cows, are continued; what doesn't exist, isn't invented. There have been many failures of formal strategic planning. In the public sector, a tragic example was the Vietnam War, despite the efforts of *The Best and The Brightest* minds.[5]

In the private sector, one of hundreds of examples was the decline of Sears Roebuck as a retailing giant despite years of strategic planning studies. Sears watched Wal-Mart, Home Depot, and other retailing innovators claim many of its previously loyal customers without a meaningful counterattack. The stock market value generation from 1985 to 1994 for Wal-Mart was $42 billion; for Home Depot, $20 billion; and for Sears, less than $1 billion.

These failures have caused strategic planning to come into some disrepute, as it has finally been recognized that planners and consultants cannot create a strategy for a company; they can only collect data, formulate hypotheses based on that data, turn the data into information, and test their ideas using standard research methods.[6] Planners cannot generate that spark of insight involving the necessary encyclopedic knowledge of a business, an industry, of technology, and of customers to concoct the next Dell Computer.

Failures of planning have been so numerous that the political scientist Aaron Wildavsky, commenting on public sector planning, suggested that planning "...has failed everywhere and at all times."[7] Because of these failures, many senior managers feel that planners have a negative impact on managerial innovation.[8] Creativity apparently diminishes under the weight of thick binders of planning documents.

---

[5] To use the title of David Halberstam's landmark history; Random House, 1972.

[6] A definitive review of the subject is Henry Mintzberg, *The Rise and Fall of Strategic Planning*, The Free Press, 1994.

[7] *The Politics of the Budgetary Process*, Little, Brown, 2nd edition, 1974, p. 205.

[8] Mansour Javidan, "Where Planning Fails – An Executive Survey," *Long Range Planning*, XVIII, 1985, pp. 89-96.

If planning has failed, why do seemingly intelligent businessmen and women pay large sums to consultants or their internal planning staffs? One possible reason is that planning allows a company to gather intelligence about itself, to regain a semblance of control of an organization possibly out of control.

Due to economies of scale requirements, the modern corporation is so large and geographically disbursed that senior management often has no clue as to what its middle managers are doing, and whether they are pursuing the vision/business strategy. Planning helps to establish a control process to derive intelligence about a company's activities.

Even HWP's Planning Fails

HWP is one of many large companies using planning advice to help plot its business strategy. HWP identified white-space opportunities to fill significant gaps in its product offerings. However, all of this planning went to naught by early 1999, when the company's vision, $HP=MC^2$, was abandoned to focus on computers and related products. The idea had been to combine measurement, computing, and communications technologies into a family of products.

But such technology initiatives as the development of new microprocessor chips and operating software was reduced, and the company became dependent on chips produced by Intel, which use some HWP technology, and Microsoft's Windows NT for its computers.[9] The new strategy is "E-services," which allows companies to rent software through the Internet and to use a new technology that will make it possible to search the Web for almost any business service.

IF SENIOR MANAGEMENT IS SO SMART, WHY AREN'T THEY RICH?

Well, they do fine from salary and stock options, but their stock market investing is additional evidence of their lack of insight about their own companies. This conclusion may be contrary to the common wisdom that corporate insiders outperform the market. For example, one publication assumes that executives know their businesses so well that their stock market decisions represent "smart money."[10]

Evidence from Publicized Stocks

However, several studies have refuted the smart money assumption in recent reports. In one brief example, a listing of six stocks by a *Forbes* columnist of at least three insider purchases and no insider sales over a six month period in early 1997 produced results which were not terribly impressive, particularly when the market in general was increasing some 20% a year over that same period; see Exhibit 4-1.

---

[9] See, Robert D. Hof, "Hewlett-Packard Made a Tough Decision, but the Right One," *Business Week*, March 15, 1999, p. 32.

[10] *Individual Investor*, February 1998, p. 54. Stock trading by insiders is reported at "www.Insider-Scores.com."

Exhibit 4-1: Insider Transactions
(during the First Half of 1997)

Company Name and Stock Symbol	Stock Price as of August 1997	Stock Price as of December 1998	Annualized % Change
Delta Financial (DFC)	$19	$5½	–60%
Fisher Scientific (FSH)	$46	$20	–46%
Invacare (IVC)	$23	$24	Nil
Polaris Industries (PII)	$30	$32	Nil
Regency Health Svcs	$15	$15[a]	Nil
Station Casinos (STN)	$7	$6	Nil

[a] Ceased trading in mid-1997.

Note: One stock on the list, Nationwide Financial Services, rose from $30/share to $51/share. Another stock, Sodak Gaming, recommended at $13, was merged into International Game Technology.

Source of recommendations: Eric S. Hardy, "The Forbes/Barra Wall Street Review, Special Focus," *Forbes Magazine*, August 11, 1997, p. 137.

The average (unweighted) loss was 18% per year over the period mid-1997 to the end of 1999, certainly an adequate period of time to implement any strategic changes contemplated by management as these shares were being acquired. One stock, Delta Financial, was trading at under $1 as of early 2001.

Research Evidence

This brief sample is too limited certainly to draw any definitive conclusions. However, research using reasonable methodology apparently bears out the inability of management to understand and take advantage of the plans of their companies.

Advisory services using insider activity for investment strategies have demonstrated mediocre performance. The *Hulbert Financial Digest* reports that *Insider Indicator* lagged the market by an average of 10% a year for three years, and is no longer published. *The Insiders* produced a 15.9% annualized return versus 17.1% for the stock market over a 13-year period. *Vickers Weekly Insider Report* beat the market on a return basis, but lagged the market on a risk-adjusted basis.[11]

The most rigorous study using all companies trading on the major exchanges over the 1975 to 1995 period reported an unimpressive result for insiders. While stocks bought by insiders do modestly outperform the market, so do stocks sold by the insiders. As the result, there is not much of a performance differential between the stocks insiders are buying and the stocks they are selling.[12]

Insiders actively trade the stock of their own companies, involving more than one-half of companies each year. However, there is very little market effect of these trades, and the "insider" stocks do not outperform the general stock indices.

---

[11] Mark Hulbert, "Insider Trading," *Forbes*, November 3, 1997, p. 402.

[12] Josef Lakonishok and Inmoo Lee, "Are Insiders' Trades Informative?" National Bureau of Economic Research Paper No. 6656, July 1998, available at "www.nber.org/papers/w6656.pdf."

INVESTMENT RIDDLES, MYSTERIES AND ENIGMAS

What we have been saying in Chapters 2 through 4 is so revolutionary and implausible that it is summarized in bold, capital letters.

SENIOR MANAGERS OF LARGE COMPANIES OFTEN DON'T KNOW WHAT IS GOING ON IN THEIR OWN ORGANIZATIONS ...

despite our preference for Newtonian order.

We desire order because organization is more preferable than chaos. Because of this desire, we put rules and boxes around groupings of human beings and assume that there is some logic to the result. Unfortunately, there is no such inevitable logic. The quality of data is generally mediocre from financial statements, through corporate intelligence systems, and in decisions involving business strategies. What Level 1 and 2 managers do know has been summarized and condensed from Level 3 through 5 reports, and then is modified and scripted for stock market consumption.

If chairmen and CEOs don't know what's going on in their companies and in their competitive environments, how likely is it that any investor can rely on management's statements regarding past results or prospects for the business? In this environment, how reliable is any investment analyst's evaluation of a company? If we can't rely on information from the company or from investment analysts, what can we use to determine the potential for company growth?

A business obviously does not manage itself in a vacuum. Senior management and the board of directors are continuously examining results in the context of generally accepted standards of performance, no matter how flawed or misleading those standards may be. As was discussed in Chapter 2, the various profitability ratios are probably the most important measures in general use, although comparisons are also made of competitors' business strategies, organizational changes, and initiatives toward profit improvement.

To summarize —

- past financial results tell us nothing useful

- earnings estimates are unreliable

- a business is an undecipherable "black box" beyond understanding to its own managers, investors, and analysts

- price and volume statistics (as used in technical analysis) are random numbers, *and*

- some stock market observers *do* beat the market (contrary to the premise in the efficient market theory).

Now that conventional wisdom has pretty much been buried, we will begin to build an approach toward 21st century stock market investing. However, be forewarned that the quantitative tools of the past will be discarded. Any insights or wisdom will result from an understanding of the progress of an industry and a company toward competing in the "new" economy.

Chapter 5

Why the E-Commerce, New Economy Changes Everything

While the law [of competition] may be sometimes hard for the individual, it is best for the race, because it insures the survival of the fittest in every department. We accept and welcome ... the concentration of business, industrial and commercial, in the hands of a few, and the law of competition between these, as being not only beneficial, but essential ...
Andrew Carnegie, *1835-1919 (American industrialist)*

Old economy business has operated under essentially the same rules and procedures for 150 years:

- the giant corporation, requiring massive capital investment

- long-term supplier and customer relationships

- a bureaucratic, generally unresponsive management structure

- decisions developed over extended time periods

- some transactions which produce only marginal profits

The double-entry accounting system used to track these business activities and calculate profits or losses has been around for some 500 (!) years, despite the many problems of judgment, allocation, and interpretation. This is all changing.

WHAT IS THE E-COMMERCE, NEW ECONOMY?

The premise of the e-commerce, new economy is global competition in industries which involve information, finance or scientific discovery. The industry groups of the new economy include computers, stock brokerage and banking, media and telecommunications, consulting, and medicine and the health professions. In contrast, the old economy has been oriented to the manufacture and distribution of product, and requires accounting for labor, raw material, and overhead inputs. New economy *thinking* instead of old economy *producing* challenges all of our established assumptions.

Core Competencies

Capital requirements will diminish as non-core competencies are eliminated. Instead of supporting interrelated manufacturing and marketing operations, companies will decide what they do better than their competitors, emphasize those activities, and outsource support functions. This will reduce the requirement for massive capital accumulation, and will allow management to emphasize profitable operations.

The resulting focus will de-emphasize horizontal and vertical business integration, reduce firm size, and alleviate organizational bureaucracy and structure. The traditional approaches to management — span of control and chain of command — will be replaced by more flexible processes stressing creativity and innovation.

Business "Relationships"

Supplier and customers will make Website offers to sell or buy. Long-time buyer/seller relationships will become secondary to global competition for markets, and cost and quality will dominate as decision factors. The entire process of selling will change, personal contact will be minimized, and many transactions will be made at the computer screen rather than over a "three martini" lunch.

Accommodations previously made for lapses or delays will be no longer be permitted, and contracts will be with the vendor that can deliver product, not baseball tickets. Favored relationships will be replaced by global competition, and organizations previously unknown in North America and Western Europe will become important business partners.

Real-Time Decisions

Decisions will be nearly real-time, occurring in hours or even minutes. In the old economy business transactions were proposed, pondered, and completed at a fairly deliberate pace, with due consideration for previous failures and successes. An important new economy characteristic is the speedy circulation of business information to all relevant parties through electronic ("e") commerce.

Managers at each participating company will be able to observe the details of each transaction and make such changes or counteroffers as seem appropriate. As the result, the established linkages between a business and its constituents will decline, and long-time relationships will be undermined through the participation of new or formerly unfamiliar companies.

Financing Costs

The potential for unprofitable decisions will exponentially increase. The financial markets have been assigning a permanently high cost to capital for the past quarter century. In the late 1960s, quality companies paid about 4% for debt (pre-tax) and about 8% for equity, comprised of a 5% annual increase in the price of publicly traded stock and a 3% dividend yield. The oil embargo of 1973-1974 triggered an explosion in financing costs, and companies today pay about 8% for debt and as much as 15% or more for equity. The impact on the weighted cost of funds is dramatic, with a near doubling of financing costs (see Exhibit 5-1).

This very real increase in the cost of funds has been accompanied by business delays in paying for goods and services. Standard credit terms used to be payment in about 30 days for most industries. However, actual average payment today is about 45 days. The result is the possibility of a planned profitable transaction turning into a loss. And new economy relationships are not likely to be as understanding if deals are poorly priced, costs are higher than expected, or shipments are delayed.

The Investor and the New Economy

As investors, we should search for companies with the drive and desire to become e-commerce "warriors." The biggest winners will come from old economy industries because they will have the largest profit opportunities. The moderate winners will be the companies which are new economy participants or provide the infrastructure for new economy businesses.

The winners will demonstrate the ability to adapt to the requirements of the new economy, while continuing to provide the essential manufacturing and distribution activities demanded by global businesses. Their motivation to change may result from several sources:

- The realization that the original selling idea of the company has reached maturity, and that competitors may erode or are eroding an entrenched industry position.

- The recognition that e-commerce changes an industry's equilibrium, and that nimble participants can seize significant market share.

- Changes to the legal or regulatory environment, enabling greater freedom of action and the ending of government-mandated prices and markets.

Exhibit 5-1: Changes in Corporate Costs of Capital

	Typical Portion of Balance Sheet	Pre-Tax Cost	After-Tax Cost[a]	Weighted After-Tax Cost[b]
Prior to 1970				
Debt	40%	0.04	0.026	0.010
Equity	60%	0.08	0.080	0.048
Total	100%			0.058
After 1970				
Debt	40%	0.08	0.053	0.021
Equity	60%	0.15	0.150	0.090
Total	100%			0.111

[a] The after-tax cost of debt is calculated as the pre-tax cost of debt times $(1 - 0.34)$, the presumed corporate income tax rate.
[b] Weighted by the typical portion of the balance sheet.

There are countless examples of businesspeople who created a superior product; sold that product until more aggressive competitors seized an important portion of their market share; and either responded and became stronger, or declined. Our interest is in those industries and companies which are being re-energized, and which have the potential and the desire to succeed in the new economic order.

The three critical factors in this search are as follows:

- industry concentration

- the extent of integrated production activities

- evidence of process innovation (as measured both by company size and EPS growth over time).

Each of these factors is described in the sections which follow.

CONCENTRATED INDUSTRIES

The first criterion is a significant degree of concentration in the industry; that is, the extent of market share controlled by the largest companies. The leading companies in concentrated industries experience oligopolistic profits as compared to their smaller competitors, more than one-third greater measured by 1999 return-on-equity (ROE) results (see Exhibit 5-2). However, all of the old economy characteristics which permit these superior results will end with the e-commerce transition.

Economic concentration is known as "oligopoly," a market situation where a few producers set terms of pricing and supply. (The buying side parallel to oligopoly, that is, where a few large companies are the only buyers and drive the terms in a transaction, is called "oligopsony." This situation is typified by the aerospace and motor vehicles industries.) Oligopolistic industries can be further classified as mature or emerging, and the drivers or motivators of each are quite different.

Emerging Oligopolies

Emerging oligopolies typically exist in industries in deregulation, such as the airlines and the banking industry. The companies in emerging oligopolies can use their resources to expand their markets and service offerings, to acquire competitors, and to fight for market share in ways not previously permitted. They are not yet sufficiently mature or concentrated to be concerned with a comprehensive e-commerce strategy.

It is typical in emerging oligopolies for prices to rise slightly faster than general price indices, or for the abandonment of products which cannot attain a "fair" return. This phenomenon occurs as companies leaving more intense competition discover that they no longer have to accept a market price, as they set (at least in part) and can raise the price to earn higher profits. They can also use their market position to negotiate lower component costs of production and distribution.

Exhibit 5-2: Return-on-Equity Results for Concentrated Industries

Fortune 500 Industry	Lgst Co.	2nd Lgst Co.	3rd Lgst Co.	4th Lgst Co.	5th Lgst Co.	6th Lgst Co.	Lgst Cos. Avg. ROE	Industry Avg. ROE	% Difference: Lgst. vs. Industry
Chemicals	60	16	11	18	11	7	20.5	15	36.7%
Computers and Office Equipment	38	19	4	31	29	21	23.7	21	12.7%
Computer Software, Services, Peripherals	27	9	35	14	26	33	24.0	16	50.0%
Network Communications and Telecommunications	4	31	35	8	26	37	23.5	11	113.6%
Forest and Paper Products	2	19	33	7	9	46	19.3	9	114.8%
Healthcare	7	29	15	12	6		11.5	6	91.7%
Pharmaceuticals	44	26	48	36		33	31.2	35	−11.0%
Rubber/Plastics	7		28	8	6	14	10.5	11	−4.5%
Scientific/Photographic	28	36	24	17		13	19.7	18	9.3%
Soaps/Cosmetics	31	51	0	16	27	15	23.3	27	−13.6%
Transportation and Equipment	30	26	17	18	17	18	21.0	18	16.7%
Total									38.0%

Notes: Calculations exclude companies with losses in 1999, and are based on unweighted return-on-equity results.

Source: Derived from data in "The Fortune 500 Issue," *Fortune Magazine*, April 17, 2000, pages F-1 through F-82.

Airlines

The airlines were controlled by the federal government (through the old Civil Aeronautics Board) until 1978, and could not compete on routes or fares. Industry deregulation has permitted competition, mergers, new airline start-ups, and private enterprise innovation in all areas except for safety issues (which is still controlled by the Federal Aviation Administration). With deregulation, airlines can raise prices, eliminate routes and hubs, and reduce such amenities as meals and legroom between seat rows.

However, competition has been painful, with industry losses of $8 billion over the most recent three-year period. This has forced the larger airlines to increase fares, cut costs, outsource some activities, reduce operations at selected airports, partner with international carriers, and manage aircraft capacity as demanded by passengers and shippers.

Banking

The U.S. banking industry included some 15,000 commercial banks as recently as the mid-1980s, primarily because of federal restrictions on interstate banking (the McFadden Act) and restrictions in some states on branch banking (i.e., Illinois). With the ending of these barriers, the commercial bank population has declined to about 9,000. When we talk about banking at the start of the 21st century, we are really addressing the 9,000 places where deposits are accepted and loans are made.

Banks today have to assign scarce dollars among several alternative choices, including merger and acquisition (M&A) activity, post M&A worker separation and site closure/integration costs, and investments in technology, employee compensation, and product and quality initiatives. Bank profits are being used more for M&A and less for other activities, with the development of technology clearly not as important as in the 1980s and 1990s.

Mature Oligopolies

Mature industries are characterized by economies of scale efficiencies. They do not face constant changes in the design of their products and services, and depend instead on incremental product improvements to retain existing customers and attract new prospects. Companies in these industries have the managerial and financial capacity to reinvent their business procedures, their production activities, and their distribution channels. They have a realistic expectation of gaining market share through more efficient manufacturing and sales processes rather than by innovations on the basic product.

There are several mature oligopolistic industries in both the "old" and "new" economies, and these are referenced in the sections which follow. One extreme situation is the automobile industry, where two U.S. based companies (General Motors and Ford) compete with the world's auto manufacturers (including DaimlerChrysler). Contrast the present situation with the state of the industry in the 1920s, when there were over 500 automobile manufacturers in the U.S. General Motors and Ford have a combined ROE of nearly 30% but are experiencing mediocre long-term growth in EPS, an annual 4%.

Challenging the Leaders

Enterprises which inhabit an oligopolistic industry are particularly vulnerable in a competitive, global e-commerce environment. Market concentration will invariably diminish as smaller American and international competitors use the Internet to sell at prices and on delivery terms which are superior to these larger, less adaptable U.S. companies.

At present, popular Internet search engines[1] cannot distinguish among vendors' offerings to satisfy buyers' required product features. Future searches based on enhanced industry specifications will uncover perhaps several dozen viable sellers which can be solicited for bids. As this occurs, the existing bonds between buyers and sellers will become obsolete, and buyers will be able to go anywhere to the best offer. Inevitably, this will lower costs, produce higher quality, and create product features which satisfy the needs of the deal.

For example, General Motors has purchased parts for its motor vehicles from the same vendors in Michigan and Indiana that it has used for decades. E-com-

---

[1] "Search engines" guide users to Internet websites based on specific inquiry criteria. Yahoo and Excite are two prominent search engines.

merce will allow new North American suppliers, and vendors in Thailand and Singapore, to bid for contracts, often at substantially lower labor rates. This is nearly a positive-sum game, with both the automobile company and the new supplier enjoying lower costs and greater profits. The loser of course is the old supplier.

Competitive Industries

Fragmented, competitive industries with many U.S. and global competitors are often not in a position to do more than fight to retain market share. They do not have the managerial or financial resources to attempt a major restructuring or to install new technology. Survival takes precedence over innovation except in the critical process of developing new products and services. See Exhibit 5-3 for a list of these industries.

Exhibit 5-3: Industries Dispersed and Unlikely to Concentrate

SIC Description and Number Reference	Shipments/ Receipts ($MM)	Degree of Concentration[a]	Earnings/ Share Growth[b]	Average ROE[c]
Food Services and Distribution (20)[d]	$134,065	44	7%	18%
Apparel and Textile Products (23)	$55,547	39	1%	14%
Industrial machinery and equipment (35)	$102,346		8%	14%
Farm machinery (3523)	$9,616	53		
Construction machinery (3531)	$13,485	53		
Metalworking machinery (354)	$26,465	31		
Special industry machinery (355)	$21,390	26		
General industrial machinery (356)	$31,390	38		
Jewelry (391)	$5,638	25	22%	16%
Total Selected Dispersed Industries	$297,596	40	7%	16%

[a] Degree of Concentration is the value added by the largest eight companies in each industry, presented as a percentage. The data are based on U.S. Department of Commerce standard industrial classification codes (SICs) used in calculating concentration ratios. Whenever two or more SICs are represented, a dollar-weighted calculation has been made of the concentration ratio. For further explanation and sources, see Exhibit 5-6.

The largest sectors are included, usually those where annual sales exceed $10 billion. Exceptions are apparel and textile products (sectors exceeding $1 billion), and printing and publishing (sectors exceeding $5 billion). Jewelry is computed from statistics for the following companies (stock symbols): DGSE, FNLY, OROA, TIF, ZLC.

[b] Average ROE is calculated by *Fortune* as net profit divided by net worth. In certain situations, calculations were made to determine the appropriate industry ROE.

[c] Average Total Return to Investors is calculated by *Fortune* as the percentage price appreciation of the common stock and the dividend yield for the period 1989-1999. In certain situations, the author made calculations to determine the appropriate industry total return to investors.

[d] Excludes mills (SIC number 207) and beverages (SIC number 208).

Source: Financial results were derived from data in "The Fortune 500 Issue," *Fortune Magazine,* April 17, 2000, pp. F-1 through F-82.

Fragmentation and competition typify wholesaling and retailing, banking, energy, insurance, and food. Admittedly, a few maverick leaders in these industries with sufficient resources and a strong market position are attempting to convert their organizations into new economy warriors. Examples include Wal-Mart (retailing) and Enron (pipelines).

Wal-Mart has created a standalone Internet unit which will feature products from every department; Internet purchases returnable to stores; the necessary mass to buy merchandise for resale at a profit (rare in the current Internet market); and a stable, quality brand name. Enron developed a $400 billion online marketplace for gas and electricity, and is expanding into bandwidth, remote data storage and other markets.

However, these companies (and a few others in fragmented, competitive industries) are the exceptions, and investors have fully priced their stock prices to reflect these innovative developments. For example, Wal-Mart sold at about 37 times reported earnings, a premium of over two times the average for all retailers. Enron sold at about 47 times, a premium of 80% for all gas, oil, and transmission companies.[2]

INTEGRATED PRODUCTION ACTIVITIES

Integrated production activities are a second required element in the selection of e-commerce industries. Integrated manufacturers typically acquire raw materials and finished components, manage complex work-in-process activities, and depend on a regular supply of high quality, cost effective components to complete their fabrication cycle. Purchasing through e-commerce is an inevitable progression toward operational efficiency, with a goal of saving 15% or 20% of the cost of manufacture.

This requirement excludes basic industries, which, by definition, are primarily in the business of converting one form of raw material to another. Basic industry examples include the smelting and extrusion of ore for aluminum and steel, and the cracking and refining of petroleum for the oil industries. These industries are not major users of acquired goods and services, and will benefit from e-commerce primarily through improved management of their raw materials and finished good inventories.

Basic industries experience more competition (50% of the value added by the eight largest companies) than those with integrated production activities (57% of the value added), generally have lower profitability, and are therefore primarily focused on competitive pressures and strategies.[3] See Exhibit 5-4 for statistics on industries demonstrating integrated production activities and Exhibit 5-5 for data on basic industries. We will return to this topic in Chapter 8.

---

[2] These statistics are as of year-end 2000.

[3] There are only limited reported statistics on basic industries, as many companies convert both raw materials and manufacture a "finished good," i.e., the oil companies. Some basic industry examples of below average growth in EPS include: building materials/glass, 2%; gas and electric utilities, 2%; and metals, −2%.

Exhibit 5-4: Manufacturing Industries Demonstrating Integrated Production Activities

SIC Description and Number Reference	Old/ New (a)	Degree of Concen- tration	Earnings/ Share Growth	Average ROE
Chemicals (281, 282, 286, 287, 289)	Old	50%	7%	15%
Computers and Office Equipment (3571, 3578, 3579)	New	60%	10%	21%
Computer Software, Services, Peripherals (3572, 3575, 3577)	New	64%	16%	16%
Forest and Paper Products (24)	Old	56%	0%	9%
Network Communications and Telecommunications, Semiconductors (366, 367)	New	50%	14%	11%
Pharmaceuticals (283)	New	50%	14%	35%
Publishing (271-274)	New	37%	6%	21%
Rubber/Plastic Products(30)	Old	48%	(2)%	11%
Scientific/Photographic Equipment(38)	New	72%	10%	17%
Soaps/Cosmetics (284)	Old	64%	11%	27%
Transportation and Equipment (37)	Old	79%	14%	18%
Total		57%	9%	18%

"Old" = old economy industry; "new" = new economy industry
For an explanation of the measures used, see Exhibit 5-3.

Exhibit 5-5: Basic Industries

SIC Description and Number Reference	Shipments/ Receipts ($MM)	Degree of Concentration
Petroleum and Coal (2911)	$136,579	49
Stone, Clay & Glass (32)	$38,777	42
Primary Metals (33)	$106,538	54
Total Basic Industries	$281,894	50

For an explanation of the measures used, see Exhibit 5-3.

At the other extreme are highly sophisticated technological industries which require safety and inspection routines too complex for e-commerce transactions. While some electronic procurement will occur, reliability and extremely tight quality control requirements will preclude any significant efficiencies through e-commerce transactions. Examples of these industries include aircraft, defense, and scientific and photographic equipment. We include such industries in our Part II discussions although the investor should be aware of the possible impediments.

The industries which meet the concentration and integrated production activities criteria are provided in Exhibit 5-3. For the convenience of the reader, the listing is in the sequence used in the Fortune 500 annual ranking. For sources on concentration data, see Exhibit 5-4.

PROCESS INNOVATION

Within these industries, there are certain companies which have demonstrated their "capacity" to innovate internal manufacturing and distribution processes. While e-commerce is primarily an information content development, it affects nearly every element in the organizational structure.[4] Transition to the new economy is measured by e-metrics, including process metrics, to determine inefficient manufacturing and marketing activities; and financial metrics using standard return ratios — return on sales and return on equity — as well as the gross margin percentage, adjusted for the time value of money (or the interest cost).

There is no single measure of innovation proficiency, and reviewing recent spending on information systems would be misleading due to corporate efforts to avoid Y2K systems problems. However, we recognize that this capability is a function both of corporate size and proven growth in the earnings per share (EPS) over an extended period of time. Companies which demonstrate these characteristics are the most likely to foster e-commerce initiatives to attain operating efficiencies and improve profitability.

Does Size Matter?

Size matters, but as a contra-indicator of e-commerce potential. While the commitment of capital and managerial talent is required, the real constraint will be the bureaucracy, unresponsiveness, and resistance of the typical large corporation. Medium-size and smaller companies typically exhibit the flexibility and inventiveness to seize on a perceived business opportunity to develop new products, adapt new technologies, and sell into new markets.

General Motors

Large companies tend to be more heavy-handed, and may pursue a strategy past the time when it has clearly failed. Nearly everyone has heard of Ford Motor's classic failure, the Edsel.[5] A more recent example of this size influence is the pressure by General Motors for participation in its electronic data interchange (EDI) initiative by its vendors. EDI uses data standards, networks, and software to enable the exchange of messages and monetary payments, eliminating the creation of paper purchase orders, invoices, mail delays and the handling of paper checks.

General Motors decided in the mid-1980s to require EDI in automating the process of ordering parts from their suppliers. Vendors were assisted in the conversion to EDI, software was supplied, a choice of intermediaries was provided to handle the transaction, and the transition was staged over a reasonable period of time. But suppliers had to eventually convert or they would be out of

---

[4] See my book *Financial and Process Metrics for the New Economy*, AMACOM Books, 2001.

[5] For the Edsel "story", see Robert F. Hartley, *Management Mistakes and Successes*, John Wiley & Sons, 1999 (6th ed.), Chapter 7. For an interesting review of other large company failures, see Robert Sobel, *When Giants Stumble: Classic Business Blunders and How to Avoid Them*, Prentice Hall, 1999.

consideration in GM purchasing decisions. Despite these efforts and GM's enormous leverage, EDI has never been a widely utilized or accepted technology.

In more recent times, this same size leverage has enabled the large motor vehicle manufacturers to develop Internet buying "hubs." A hub does a software search for specific "markers" to find competitive products meeting specific purchasing criteria. E-commerce solicitations can be posted to secure bids meeting the buying company's requirements. The efforts and leverage of the big auto manufacturers may succeed this time in what seems like a reasonable idea, but smaller global auto companies may strike better deals, attain lower prices, and enjoy more flexibility in purchasing decisions.

Other Industry "Leaders"

The leading companies in their industries often are no longer the superior performers that their smaller followers attempt to emulate. In 2000 several industry leaders experienced major structural changes or a sudden CEO departure, including AT&T, Honeywell, Coca-Cola, Proctor & Gamble, Gillette, Eastman Kodak, and Xerox. These were the ascendant companies for decades, but made bad bets on technology (AT&T: cable and high-speed Internet access); on product innovation (Gillette: battery technology); on marketing (Proctor & Gamble: competition from private-label brands); or on other elements of their business strategy.

Creative Destruction

These situations illustrate the notion that the largest companies in an industry are not necessarily the smartest, the most profitable, or the best innovators. It is more likely that their leaner challengers will have the flexibility to respond to changing economic conditions, to make return expectations of investors, and to creatively destruct[6] older business and grow newer, more competitive ones.

The application of these concepts has expanded in recent years to include both previously protected (i.e., regulated) monopolies and oligopolies, and global competitors.

- Regulated industries are rapidly losing their protected status. The airlines, public utilities, the securities industry, and banking are a few examples. In those cases management had a more-or-less "free ride," although pricing was set by an external controlling body, i.e, a state public service commission. Today those companies are being forced to learn to compete or lose investor interest.[7]

---

[6] "Creative destruction" was a concept of Harvard economist Joseph Schumpeter (1883-1950); see *Capitalism, Socialism and Democracy*, New York: Harper, 1942, Chapter 7. However, Schumpeter believed that capitalism would eventually become redundant as technology became institutionalized and management became bureaucratic. He foresaw the failure of capitalism and an eventual migration to socialism, which obviously has not occurred.

[7] For example, AT&T was selling in the 50s in early 2000, and as of this writing (early 2001) is in the low 20s. Investors have apparently concluded that expansion into cable and high-speed Internet businesses at a cost of $100 billion was a questionable strategy when facing wireless competition. See, David Leonhardt, "The Chaos at the Core of Prosperity," *The New York Times*, November 5, 2000, §III, pp. 1, 13.

- Global competitors are appearing from everywhere on the Internet, and with lower labor costs than the U.S. or European Union countries, and adherence to established quality standards (i.e., ISO 9000), are able to disrupt long-established buyer-seller relationships.

The result is intense competition, primarily through innovation on product features and, secondarily, on pricing. This reality is forcing business to make large bets on unproven technology, to squeeze costs by outsourcing activities that are not core competencies and by massive staff downsizing, and to endure constant senior management changes.

The essential fact about capitalism is the dynamic development of new forms and structures that continually change the economic structure from within. While price competition is important, the competitive drive is derived from innovation on technological concepts as applied to existing products and services. And those changes have historically come from the hungrier companies, those which are not number one, two or three but want to be.

Corporate Size and the Law

The U.S. Department of Justice is charged with the responsibility of administering the various antitrust laws enacted by Congress. The most publicized prosecution in recent years has certainly been against Microsoft.[8] However, other mergers of industry leaders have *not* been challenged; some examples include Citigroup/Travelers Insurance, DaimlerChrysler, ExxonMobil and AOL/Time Warner.[9]

This benign attitude possibly stems from the government's realization that size is no longer a determinant of market control. In fact, legal experts are no longer certain what constitutes malevolent restraint of trade (although monopolies will almost certainly continue to be considered as against public policy).[10]

Do Earnings Matter?

Growth in EPS is a useful measure as a constant and objective result which best reflects a company's efforts at developing efficiencies. We noted in Chapter 3 that investors make two major mistakes concerning a stock market investment:

1. They focus on the latest reported quarterly earnings. Profit results can easily be managed in the short-term to meet or exceed Wall Street expecta-

---

[8] See "Conclusions of Law," in *U.S. vs. Microsoft* (2000), in "Company Found to Have Abused Monopoly Power," *The New York Times*, April 4, 2000, pp. C14-C15. The district court found that the company monopolized the operating systems market by "...a deliberate assault upon entrepreneurial efforts that ... could well have enabled the introduction of competition..." (at Section I.A.III.C., page C15). The decision is being appealed by Microsoft.

[9] See the discussion in Louis Uchitelle, "Who's Afraid No That Big is No Longer Bad?" *The New York Times*, November 5, 2000, §3, pp. 1, 12.

[10] Provisions of the Sherman Act of 1890 prohibit the restraint of trade (section 1) and monopoly (section 2), as amended by the Clayton Act of 1914.

tions, and there is ample evidence of such manipulation by major companies. These types of charges make it nearly impossible to know "true" earnings at any given time.

2. They use the total return results (the growth and dividend yield) to choose among investment alternatives. However, total return is measured on past results, and not the future, because we cannot know next year's stock price performance, the growth portion.

Average ROE may vary in any given year due to competitive or economic pressures, management successes or mistakes, or other factors. EPS growth measured over a representative period of time overcomes these deficiencies, and demonstrates a company's commitment to continual internal improvements and actions to manage costs.

IF IT WERE EASY, EVERYONE WOULD BE RICH

Stock market investing in the second part of the 20th century was relatively simple: computing price-earnings ratios, tracking growth in earnings per share, charting share price or volume trends, or simply buying a portfolio of stocks (i.e., a mutual fund) with an acceptable risk profile (or Beta). After the Second World War, the U.S. economy was pulled along by global demand for old and new economy products and services, and you could buy most stocks and eventually make money.

Investing in this century requires a new strategy, one which does not depend on simplistic quantitative analysis. Instead, stock selection will now involve several interrelated factors, the totality of which will indicate the ability and will of a company to successfully compete in the e-commerce, new economy. We've outlined several such factors in this chapter: the degree of industrial concentration, the use of integrated production activities, and evidence of process innovation.

One other caveat: It should be obvious from your reading of Chapters 1 through 4 that no quantitative routine can be mechanically applied to stock market investing. Specific circumstances may intercede to make an industry or a company unattractive despite meeting the various criteria discussed in this chapter. For example, the recent automobile tire recall problem facing Bridgestone/Firestone and other companies must be considered when choosing an investment. Similarly, the antitrust decision by the U.S. district court in the Microsoft case should be considered in any decision to invest in Microsoft shares.

Exhibit 5-6: SIC Sources

The Standard Industrial Classification (SIC) data used in determining economic concentration is based on the most recent statistics published by the U.S. Department of Commerce, as taken from the 1992 Economic Census, *Census of Manufactures*, and published as table MC92-S-2, "Concentration Ratios in Manufacturing." Other reports from that census containing concentration data include the following:

- Financial, Insurance and Real Estate Industries, report FC92-S-1
- Retail Trade, report RC92-S-1
- Service Industries, report SC92-S-1
- Transportation, Communications and Utilities, report UC92-S-1
- Wholesale Trade, report WC92-S-1

Existing SICs are being replaced by the North American Industry Classification System (NAICS). According to the U.S. Department of Commerce, NAICS makes substantial structural improvements and identifies over 350 new industries. The NAICS process reorganizes the classification system on a more consistent economic principle — based on types of production activities performed — rather than the mixture of production-based and market-based categories in the SIC. This will allow for the presentation of more detail for the rapidly expanding service sector that accounts for most economic activity but only 40 percent of SIC categories. Further, the system was redefined jointly with Canada and Mexico so that comparable statistics could be obtained for the three NAFTA trading partners.

NAICS groups the economy into 20 broad sectors, up from the 10 divisions of the SIC system. Many of the new sectors reflect recognizable parts of SIC divisions, such as the Utilities and Transportation sectors, broken out from the SIC division Transportation, Communications, and Utilities. Similarly, the SIC division for Service Industries has been subdivided to form several new sectors with longer names: Professional, Scientific and Technical Services; Management, Support, Waste Management, and Remediation Services; Education Services; Health and Social Assistance; Arts, Entertainment, and Recreation; and Other Services except Public Administration.

Other sectors represent combinations of pieces from more than one SIC division. The new Information sector includes major components from Transportation, Communications, and Utilities (broadcasting and telecommunications), Manufacturing (publishing), and Services Industries (software publishing, data processing, information services, motion picture and sound recording). The Accommodation and Food Services sector puts together hotels and other lodging places from Service Industries and eating and drinking places from Retail Trade.

NAICS industries are identified by a 6-digit code, in contrast to the 2, 3, and 4-digit SIC code. The longer code accommodates the larger number of sectors and allows more flexibility in designating sub-sectors. It also provides for additional detail not necessarily appropriate for all three NAICS countries. The international NAICS agreement fixes only the first five digits of the code. The sixth digit, where used, identifies subdivisions of NAICS industries that accommodate user needs in individual countries. Thus, 6-digit U.S. codes may differ from counterparts in Canada or Mexico, but at the 5-digit level they are standardized.

Some of these industries reflect "high tech" developments such as fiber optic cable manufacturing, satellite communications, and the reproduction of computer software. Others recognize less technological changes in the way business is done, such as environmental consulting, credit card issuing, and satellite communications. In addition, there will be numerous new retailing categories.

Manufacturing and business service industries which will be separately recognized for the first time by NAICS include:

Semiconductor machinery manufacturing	Telecommunication resellers
Fiber optic cable manufacturing	Credit card issuers
Reproduction of computer software	Temporary help
Manufacture of compact discs	Telemarketing bureaus
Cable networks	Industrial design services
Satellite communications	Hazardous waste collection
Paging	HMO medical centers
Cellular/wireless communications	

Part II

The Winners and the Losers

Come, Watson, come! The game is afoot.
Sir Arthur Conan Doyle, *1859–1930 (The Return of Sherlock Holmes)*

In Part II we discuss the industries and companies which constitute the big winners, the moderate winners, and the losers in stock market investing.

- The *big winners* (see Chapter 6) are the 25 industrial and service companies which will benefit to the greatest extent from ongoing e-commerce and new economy initiatives.

- The *moderate winners* (see Chapter 7) are the 25 information and cash/financial infrastructure companies on which the success of the big winners will be based.

- The *losers* (see Chapter 8) are those industries and companies unable or unwilling to adjust to the changing requirements of 21st century competition.

Because specific industries and companies are reviewed in these three chapters, a note on methodology is included prior to embarking on our analysis. Although the procedures for selecting industries (discussed in Chapter 5) do not change over time, new data will be published concerning concentration statistics. Furthermore, financial results will change each year regarding the performance of companies and earnings over time. It is therefore essential to understand that the process will periodically result in revisions to our stock selections.

It should also be noted that the assignment of a company to an industry, and indeed, the nomenclature and description of each industry, will vary by the standard reference cited. For example, General Electric is identified as a diversified financial company in the "Fortune 500" listing; as a movies and home entertainment company by Standard & Poor's; and as a conglomerate by *Business Week*. For the sake of consistency and reader convenience, we use the "Fortune 500" assignments.

In the industry tables in the next three chapters, the corporations listed in **boldface** in the exhibits meet both the ranking and EPS growth criteria, and are *not* the largest enterprises in their industries. Companies whose ownership changed during 2000 due to a merger or acquisition are included as a part of the surviving organization. For sources, see the Appendix to Part II.

Chapter 6

The Big Winners

Winning isn't everything, it's the only thing.
Vince Lombardi *(Attributed), 1913-1970*
(National Football League coach)

Everyone is looking for the big stock market winners. How do we find them? Based on everything we've discussed so far, we won't be looking in the *Business Week* quarterly Corporate Scoreboard, the *Barron's* "Market Laboratory" statistical section, or *The Wall Street Journal*'s list of price-earnings ratios. Instead, we will be looking for specific evidence of responsiveness to the demands of the e-commerce, new economy.

ATTRIBUTES OF THE BIG WINNERS

In Chapter 5 we reviewed the attributes of big winners in the e-commerce, new economy: significant industry concentration, integrated production activities, and evidence of process innovation (as measured both by company size and EPS growth over time). Companies in industries with these properties can make or are making the necessary transition to the economic order of the third millennium. Their shareholders will be the primary beneficiaries of the e-commerce transition.

We eliminated basic industries; emerging oligopolies; fragmented, competitive industries; and highly technological, safety-oriented products and services. We focused instead on profitable companies in mature oligopolies with integrated processing. The 25 companies with both attributes (size and EPS growth) demonstrate the possibility of a successful conversion to e-commerce.

It is critical to understand that the industries and companies discussed in this chapter represent established industries, but only those with the proven capability to institute new economy processes. A few examples:

- The chemical industry epitomizes the old economy, tracing its founding in the U.S. to the DuPont Company in 1802. However, Internet hubs (e.g., ChemConnect and CheMatch) created to match buyers and sellers of chemical products make the industry very much a part of the new economy.

- The transportation industry, in existence since the American Revolution, has completely remade itself to support just-in-time (JIT) purchasing initiatives and to deliver business and consumer products to buyers.

- The health care industry is remaking itself — albeit very painfully and slowly — with EDI (electronic data interchange) and e-commerce protocols to automate administrative activities and eliminate a substantial portion of costs.

In the sections which follow, we discuss these industries and "winner" companies.

OLD ECONOMY INDUSTRIES

The old economy industries which will be big winners are chemicals, forest and paper products, rubber and plastic products, soaps and cosmetics, and transportation and related equipment.

Chemicals

The chemicals industry constitute one of the largest group of U.S. companies by dollar revenues at $465 billion (1999 figures). However, the industry has had a somewhat unusual structure, with some very large participants shipping an annual $5 billion or more (primarily basic chemical companies like DuPont and Dow), and numerous smaller companies shipping about $1 billion or less each year (primarily specialty chemical companies). Sales in the industry have been increasing at about the rate of general economic growth while profits have been mediocre.

Structural changes are beginning to drive efficiencies, including the globalization of sales and manufacturing, cost reduction initiatives, consolidation through merger and acquisition activity, and a re-focus on core competencies. The U.S. market is generally considered as mature, with the largest growth likely to be in developing countries. This will encourage the construction of indigenous production facilities, particularly given the lower cost structure for land and labor.

As some half of all chemical industry production is essential raw material for other U.S. manufacturing, e-commerce initiatives will also drive profitability through improved information on purchasing requirements and specifications, shipping dates and modes, and pricing. Chemical e-commerce transactions are estimated to be in the hundreds of billions of dollars in the next few years. Connectivity will occur through hubs (defined in Chapter 5), dedicated company sites, and cooperative sites operated by several companies, with products, integrated solutions and contract sales. Chemical companies ranked by revenue and growth in EPS are listed in Exhibit 6-1.

Forest and Paper Products

Like chemicals, forest and paper products constitute one of the largest industries in the U.S. In the past, domestic and global economic trends drove a cyclicality which led to difficult supply and demand balancing and significant profitability variations. However, the international potential is huge, given the significantly higher usage of paper and paperboard by developed economies, often by a factor of ten to twelve times.

Exhibit 6-1: Chemical Companies

Companies Ranked by Revenue	Companies Ranked by EPS Growth
DuPont	Ecolab
Dow Chemical	Cabot
PPG Industries	DuPont
Union Carbide	Valspar
Rohm & Haas	**Sherwin-Williams**
Air Products & Chemicals	H.B. Fuller
Sherwin-Williams	Sigma-Aldrich
Praxair	RPM
Eastman Chemical	**Avery Dennison**
Engelhard	**Air Products & Chemicals**
FMC	Ferro
Avery Dennison	Lubrizol

Exhibit 6-2: Forest and Paper Products Companies

Companies Ranked by Revenue	Companies Ranked by EPS Growth
International Paper	Chesapeake
Georgia-Pacific	Bemis
Kimberly-Clark	Kimberly-Clark
Weyerhaeuser	Sonoco Products
Smurfit-Stone Container	Weyerhaeuser
Fort James	**Williamette Industries**
Boise Cascade	**Louisiana-Pacific**
Williamette	**Mead**
Temple-Inland	Georgia-Pacific
Mead	Temple-Inland
Louisiana-Pacific	Fort James

As the U.S. portion of the industry matures, it has experienced some consolidation, allowing improved management of administrative costs and capacity. Significant mergers include James River and Ft. Howard merger (to form Ft. James Corp., 1997), Bowater/Avenor (1998), Jefferson Smurfit/Stone Container (1998), International Paper (IP)/Union Camp (1999)/Champion International (1999), and Weyerhauser/MacMillan Bloedel (1999). Recent divestitures of non-core businesses were completed by IP, Champion Paper, Louisiana-Pacific, Mead and Boise-Cascade.

The industry has worked to accommodate various environmental restrictions, including the preservation of virgin forests and wildlife, and the air and water pollution resulting from the manufacture of paper products. A major initiative has been the recycling of paper fibers, which can be reused many times to produce paper and containerboard products. Another alternative is engineered wood made from wood residue or readily available small diameter logs, which are not subject to ecological controls. Forest and paper products companies ranked by revenue and growth in EPS are listed in Exhibit 6-2.

Exhibit 6-3: Rubber/Plastic Products Companies

Companies Ranked by Revenue	Companies Ranked by EPS Growth
Goodyear Tire	**Carlisle**
Pactiv	**Cooper Tire**
Sealed Air	
M.A. Hanna	
Cooper Tire	
Gencorp	
Carlisle	
Foamex International	

Rubber and Plastic Products

Rubber and plastic are component materials in the automotive and transportation industries. Principal sectors and companies include the following:

- Original equipment manufacturers ("OEM"): Johnson Controls, TRW, Goodyear Tire and Rubber, Bridgestone/Firestone, Dana, Magna International

- Replacement or aftermarket: Federal-Mogul, Arvin, Exide, Cooper Tire

- Parts distribution: Genuine Parts, Republic Automotive Parts

- Rubber fabricators: Cooper Tire, Michelin (France)

As with the other old economy industries, intensifying global competition is forcing aggressive programs to enhance productivity and efficiency. These actions are also being driven by cost pressures from the major automobile manufacturers, which have announced their own plans to create a buying hub for auto parts. Furthermore, the automobile industry and certain of its tire suppliers have been severely impacted by the recent Firestone problems with peeling tire treads primarily used on Ford sport-utility vehicles.

There are various rubber and plastic applications other than the automotive and transportation industries. These include component systems for the construction industry, such as roofing materials, membranes, pipes, siding and appliances; the industrial market, consisting of gaskets, seals, hoses, belts and similar products; and plastic compounds and resins used in protective, food and specialty packaging products. Rubber and plastic products companies ranked by revenue and growth in EPS are listed in Exhibit 6-3.

Soaps and Cosmetics

Soaps and cosmetics are a sector within consumer nondurables, and include household products (such as cleaners, detergents and additives, and various kitchen items) and personal care (cosmetics, fragrances, oral care, soap, and hair and skin care). The industry's economics are driven by population growth and household formation, which have been slowing in the U.S.

As the result, companies are attempting to develop efficient international marketing strategies, led primarily by Unilever, Proctor & Gamble, and Colgate-Palmolive, which have been experiencing competitive pressures from smaller companies. Such efforts include extending the use of products to cultures which may be susceptible to greater sales efforts, pricing responsively to competition from private labels, and increased product introductions. New initiatives increase total sales while supporting more attractive profit margins than entrenched brands.

The brand management concept predominant in the second half of the 20th century will likely be replaced by a few global brands. Global brand marketing will enhance retail store shelf space allocations, reduce the costs of production, and allow the extension of product lines through innovative differentiation. Declining product lines will be discarded, and there are already companies buying abandoned brands (i.e., Oxydol, sold to Redox Brands). Soaps and cosmetics companies ranked by revenue and growth in EPS are listed in Exhibit 6-4.

Transportation and Related Equipment

Few industries personify the old economy more than transportation, including motor vehicles, airlines, transportation equipment, and trucking. The component industries of the manufacturing sector could not move to points of further assembly or to final markets without an efficient transportation system. Fortunately, operational procedures established more than a century ago have begun to segue into new economy techniques, particularly just-in-time (JIT) and economic order quantity (EOQ) routines which require daily deliveries of materiel.

Less-than-truckload (LTL) freight is the critical element in the new economy. LTL provides daily infusions of inventory for manufacturing and assembly, and supplies new retailing merchandise. Truckload motor carriers and the railroads should experience growth at approximately the rate as the global economy, although a long-term rise in energy costs or labor instability will clearly impact profits.

Exhibit 6-4: Soaps/Cosmetics Companies

Companies Ranked by Revenue	Companies Ranked by EPS Growth
Proctor & Gamble	Avon Products
Colgate-Palmolive	Colgate-Palmolive
Avon Products	Proctor & Gamble
Clorox	**Alberto-Culver**
Estee Lauder	**Clorox**
Alberto-Culver	Intl. Flavors & Fragrances
Revlon	
Dial	
Intl. Flavors & Fragrances	

Exhibit 6-5: Transportation and Equipment Companies

Companies Ranked by Revenue	Companies Ranked by EPS Growth
AMR	Harley-Davidson
UAL	Arvin Industries
TRW	**Navistar International**
Johnson Controls	Trinity Industries
Delta Air Lines	Johnson Controls
Dana	**Eaton**
Lear	Mascotech
NWA	Federal-Mogul
Paccar	Oashkosh Truck
Navistar International	**Paccar**
Eaton	**Dana**
	TRW

LTL is integrated into bulk transportation industries through intermodal facilities. The completion of the Conrail split (to CSX and Norfolk Southern) and the 1996 Union Pacific/Southern Pacific acquisition will lead to greater railroad efficiencies and improved service to shippers. Rail will also be promoted as the result of the NAFTA promotion of Canadian-U.S.-Mexican manufacturing opportunities.

Various companies provide technological systems in support of this industry, such as hydraulics, control, and drivetrain systems. Recent growth has been hampered by efforts to extend the usage of existing capital equipment. E-commerce will reduce inventories of parts, reduce reliance on distributors for orders, and develop closer relationships between buyers and sellers. Transportation and equipment companies ranked by revenue and growth in EPS are listed in Exhibit 6-5.

Other Industries

Certain other old economy industries are transitioning to new product lines and manufacturing processes. Two examples:

- Metal products companies, now variously assigned to household durables and nondurables, homebuilding and other specialized industries

- Electronics and electrical products companies, classified as network communications and telecommunications, household durables, aerospace, semiconductors and other specialized industries

Because of this evolution, we will not be reviewing metal products or electronics and electrical products.

Old Economy Companies

Within old economy industries, the companies meeting our criteria include three chemical companies, five in forest and paper products, two in rubber and plastics, two in soaps and cosmetics, and five in transportation and equipment.

Company/ Symbol/Beta	Industry	Sales (millions)	Principal Company Businesses
Air Products & Chemicals (APD)/0.90	Chemicals	$5,467.1 (FY 2000)	Gases for the chemical, steel, electronics, oil and food industries; various chemical intermediaries; specialty integrated gas processing
Avery Dennison (AVY)/0.90	Chemicals	$3,768.2 (FY 1999)	Self adhesive office and factory materials; specialty chemicals; sales in 30 countries
Sherwin-Williams (SHW)/0.95	Chemicals	$5,003.8 (FY 1999)	Largest North American producer of paints and varnishes; also manufactures application equipment and transportation coatings; owns/operates 2,300 stores
Kimberly-Clark (KMB)/0.70	Forest and Paper Products	$13,007.0 (FY 1999)	Natural and synthetic fiber-based products for personal, business and industrial uses, including Kleenex and Scott, Huggies and Kotex
Louisiana-Pacific (LPX)/0.85	Forest and Paper Products	$3,488.2 (FY 1999)	Building products including structural panels, lumber, engineered wood and wood fiber
Mead (MEA)/1.00	Forest and Paper Products	$3,799.5 (FY 1999)	Coated and specialty papers, paperboard, packaging, corrugating materials, office and consumer products
Weyerhaeuser (WY)/1.20	Forest and Paper Products	$12,262.0 (FY 1999)	Timber-growing and real estate activities, and forest products including pulp; plywood; strand, container and particle-board; newsprint; papers
Williamette (WLL)/1.05	Forest and Paper Products	$4,078.0 (FY 1999)	Diverse forest products company, including brown and finished papers, containers, linerboard, bags, sacks, plywood, lumber, particleboard
Carlisle (CSL)/0.90	Rubber and Plastics	$1,611.3 (FY 1999)	Components manufacturer for construction, industry, transportation and other markets
Cooper Tire (CTB)/1.00	Rubber and Plastics	$2,196.3 (FY 1999)	Primarily replacement tires for vehicles, although 30% of sales are engineering rubber products
Alberto-Culver (ACV)/0.85	Soaps and Cosmetics	$1,975.9 (FY 1999)	Consumer personal care, including beauty, hair and skin products
Clorox (CLX)/0.90	Soaps and Cosmetics	$4,003.0 (FY 1999)	Household products, including cleaning, bleach and food preparation
Dana (DCN)/1.10	Transportation and Equipment	$13,217.0 (FY 1999)	OEM and aftermarket manufacturing
Eaton (ETN)/0.80	Transportation and Equipment	$8,402.0 (FY 1999)	Engineered products for industrial, transportation, construction and semiconductor markets and electrical power distribution
Navistar International (NAV)/1.25	Transportation and Equipment	$8,647.0 (FY 1999)	Truck manufacturing, diesel engines and the financing of these products
Paccar (PCAR)/1.05	Transportation and Equipment	$9,021.0 (FY 1999)	Manufacture of trucks and related aftermarket distribution of parts, and finance and leasing services
TRW (TRW)/0.85	Transportation and Equipment	$16,969.0 (FY 1999)	Products for the transportation industry including steering, suspension and restraint systems; also aerospace and information technology systems

NEW ECONOMY INDUSTRIES

The new economy industries which will be big winners are health care, pharmaceuticals, scientific/photographic equipment, and leisure and entertainment. Others not specifically discussed in this chapter are diversified outsourcing, electronics and electrical equipment, mail/package/freight delivery, temporary help, and waste management.

Health Care

The health care industry, the largest sector in the U.S. economy at about $1.25 trillion, has struggled for years from a multitude of problems. These include inadequate returns; physician, nursing, and patient complaints about service problems; a maze of governmental regulation and oversight; rising medical expenses, particularly the cost of drugs; inadequate Medicare reimbursement for policyholder treatment; and few new opportunities to expand coverage to paying clients.

Without a political consensus on a comprehensive approach to these problems, there may be no alternative but the continued rationing of health care by provider organizations, increases in monthly premiums, and industry consolidation to eliminate redundant administrative costs. The recent merger of Aetna U.S. Healthcare/Prudential will likely lead to the consolidation of smaller HMOs into large national organizations, such as CIGNA and United Healthcare.

E-commerce will be the next generation of efficiency, replacing EDI formats now in limited use. With administrative costs variously estimated between 10% to 18% of health care costs, e-commerce can be used for various paper-intensive tasks. These include capturing enrollment data; exchanging medical information, including coverages; speeding referrals between health professionals; submitting claim reimbursement requests; ordering supplies and equipment; and tracking epidemiological statistics on patterns of disease. Health care organizations ranked by revenue and growth in EPS are listed in Exhibit 6-6.

Exhibit 6-6: Health Care Companies

Companies Ranked by Revenue	Companies Ranked by EPS Growth
Aetna	Unitedhealth Group
CIGNA	Universal Health
Unitedhealth Group	Omnicare
Columbia/HCA	CIGNA
Tenet Healthcare	**Humana**
Humana	Healthsouth
Foundation Health Systems	
Wellpoint Health Networks	
Anthem Insurance	
Caremark RX	
Express Scripts	

Exhibit 6-7: Pharmaceutical Companies

Companies Ranked by Revenue	Companies Ranked by EPS Growth
Merck	Bristol-Myers Squibb
Johnson & Johnson	**Schering-Plough**
Bristol-Myers Squibb	Pfizer
Pfizer	Merck
American Home Products	Warner-Lambert
Abbott Labs	Johnson & Johnson
Warner-Lambert	**Abbott Labs**
Eli Lilly	Allergan
Schering-Plough	**Eli Lilly**
Pharmacia & Upjohn	Pharmacia & Upjohn

Pharmaceuticals

The pharmaceutical industry, a $375 billion industry, has experienced ideal conditions for growth in recent years, with innovative new drugs, faster Food and Drug Administration approvals, and a desire to substitute medications and medical devices for hospital stays. Recent drug introductions include medications for cholesterol management, arthritis, irritable bowel syndrome, and hypertension. New introductions are expected of about 1,000 new drugs for cancer, heart disease, AIDS and mental illness, and will involve inhalation, transdermal and gene therapy delivery systems.

The principal negatives are the impending expirations for numerous drugs, which will lead to cheaper, generic versions; and the possibility of more active governmental involvement in controlling prescription costs. Pressure on traditional distribution channels is developing through direct to consumer advertising and Internet retailing.

The industry is actively pursuing merger opportunities to reduce production and marketing costs. Recent transactions include Pfizer/Warner-Lambert (2000), Pharmacia & Upjohn/Monsanto (2000), Astra AB/Zeneca (1999), Sanofi/Synthelabo (1999), and a possible merger involving SmithKline Beecham and Glaxo Wellcome. In addition, strategic alliances are developing for promotion, cross-licensing, research and development, and production. Pharmaceutical companies ranked by revenue and growth in EPS are listed in Exhibit 6-7.

Scientific/Photographic Equipment

Scientific products include the manufacturing and distribution of laboratory and hospital/medical provider devices. Recent innovations include cardiovascular devices; blood and kidney procedures; stents for vascular intervention; defibrillators for irregular heartbeats; and laser surgery techniques.

The industry will continue to prosper due to these and other technological developments; the aging of the population; the desire to avoid lengthy hospital stays; and the continued government stalemate on major policy changes and cost containment. However, pricing pressures are likely to increase due to HMO pressure, hospital consolidation, and the development of procurement hubs through the Internet.

Exhibit 6-8: Scientific/Photographic Equipment

Companies Ranked by Revenue	Companies Ranked by EPS Growth
3M	Teradyne
Eastman Kodak	**Applied Materials**
Baxter Intl.	**Bausch & Lomb**
Applied Materials	**Medtronic**
Thermo Electron	Perkin-Elmer
Medtronic	Eastman Kodak
Becton Dickinson	Beckman Coulter
Boston Scientific	
Mallinckrodt	
Guidant	
Bausch & Lomb	
Stryker	

The old photographic/image capture business pioneered by Eastman Kodak is being rapidly replaced by repositioning (or "repurposing"), including the swapping, manipulating, storing, and displaying of digital images. These opportunities allow commercial and personal users to adapt photographic technology to a variety of applications, including medical and scientific, business, engineering, and entertainment.

Historically, most of the revenue of these companies was derived from such nondurable components as film, chemicals and paper. Kodak's competitors include traditional photography companies like Fuji, and newer technologies sold by Hewlett-Packard, Sony and other electronics, technology and Internet photo processing companies. Scientific and photographic equipment companies ranked by revenue and growth in EPS are listed in Exhibit 6-8.

Leisure and Entertainment

The leisure and entertainment industry is "new economy" as it is primarily the result of intellectual property, and in our definition, includes movies, home entertainment (as broadly defined), and gaming. For certain of these sectors, the cost structure requires huge fixed investments in each new endeavor, forcing the industry to partner, cross-promote, and seek new global distribution channels.

Merger and acquisition activity will continue as larger companies attempt to integrate the principal leisure pursuits, such as personal computer, Internet, movie and home entertainment (including network and cable television). Recent transactions include AOL/Time Warner (2000), Viacom/CBS (1999), NBC (General Electric)/Paxson Communications (1999), and Walt Disney/Capital Cities ABC (1996). To partially offset rising expenses, ticket prices and fees will continue to rise.

The double-digit growth in the gaming/casino business has somewhat abated, although the industry is generating $30 billion in revenues annually. Capacity has significantly increased in most venues where gaming is legal, with Las Vegas now offering some 125,000 rooms and several new casinos, and consolidation will affect the gaming business as operators seek to control costs, gain geographic diversification, and link collateral pastimes (i.e., horse racing, movies with "action" themes, amusement parks) to casino activities.

Exhibit 6-9: Leisure and Entertainment

Companies Ranked by Revenue	Companies Ranked by EPS Growth
Time Warner	**Hasbro**
Walt Disney	Walt Disney
Viacom	MGM Grand
Marriott Intl.	Hilton
CBS	
Mattel	
Starwood Hotels	
Cendant	
Hasbro	

Our broad definition of home entertainment includes the toy industry, which is undergoing a double transformation: problems in traditional toy outlets (like Toys "R" Us) and the rise of general discounters (i.e., Wal-Mart); and sales through the Internet. The resulting competitive business model is requiring new strategies to tie-in to other media (such as movies and television characters), extend toy cycles through phased introductions of characters (such as Beanie Babies and Barbie), and the design of interactive, electronics using microchip technology. Leisure and entertainment companies ranked by revenue and growth in EPS are listed in Exhibit 6-9.

NEW ECONOMY COMPANIES

Within new economy industries, the companies meeting our criteria include one in health care, three pharmaceutical companies, three producing scientific/photographic equipment, and one in leisure/entertainment.

Company/ Symbol/Beta	Industry	Sales (millions)	Principal Company Businesses
Humana (HUM)/1.15	Health Care	$10,113.0 (FY 1999)	Large and small group commercial, Medicare and Medicaid business insurance (including dental, life, disability)
Abbott Labs (ABT)/0.70	Pharmaceuticals	$13,177.6 (FY 1999)	Health care and diagnostics, pharmaceutical and hospital products and services
Eli Lilly (LLY)/0.40	Pharmaceuticals	$10,002.9 (FY 1999)	Pharmaceutical products including cancer treatments, anti-depressants, antibiotics, growth hormones, anti-ulcer agents and cardiovascular therapy
Schering-Plough (SGP)/0.80	Pharmaceuticals	$9,176.0 (FY 1999)	Pharmaceutical and health care products, including prescription drugs, animal health and various over-the-counter remedies
Applied Materials (AMAT)/2.30	Scientific/Photographic Equipment	$9,564.0 (FY 2000)	Semiconductor wafer fabrication equipment and parts; metrology systems and inspection equipment

Company/ Symbol/Beta	Industry	Sales (millions)	Principal Company Businesses
Bausch & Lomb (BOL)/0.40	Scientific/Photographic Equipment	$1,756.1 (FY 1999)	Healthcare products for the eye including vision care, pharmaceuticals and surgical equipment
Medtronic (MDT)/0.75	Scientific/Photographic Equipment	$5,015.0 (FY 2000)	Medical technology for cardiac rhythm management and neurological, and spinal, vascular and cardiac surgery
Hasbro (HAS)/0.90	Leisure and Entertainment	$4,232.3 (FY 1999)	Markets toy products, games, infant and pre-school items, and dolls, including G.I. Joe, Tonka, Nerf balls, *Pokemon*, *Scrabble* and *Monopoly*

FINAL THOUGHTS ABOUT THE BIG WINNERS

To recap, there are 25 potential "warrior" companies, 17 in the old economy and 8 in the new economy. Some of these are acknowledged leaders in their industries and can be found in many portfolios, such as the three pharmaceutical companies. Others are often considered as "aging" and struggling to overcome problems: Air Products & Chemicals and Cooper Tire come to mind. However, in a diversified portfolio, these are the stocks which will produce the big wins in the transition to e-commerce.

Chapter 7
The Moderate Winners

*Even if he is mediocre, there are a lot of mediocre judges
and people and lawyers. They are entitled to a little repre-
sentation, aren't they, and a little chance? We can't all have
Brandeises, Cardozos and Frankfurters and stuff like that
there.*
Roman Hruska, *1904-1999 (U.S. Senator defending Pres-
ident Richard Nixon's proposed 1970 appointment of G.
Harrold Carswell to the Supreme Court)*

In the coming decade, the moderate winners will be those companies which provide the infrastructure for the exchange of information and cash. For information, the industries are computers and office equipment; computer software, services and peripherals; network communications and telecommunications; and semiconductors. For cash, this includes banks; diversified financial companies and securities firms; and insurance companies.

INFRASTRUCTURE CYCLES

An *infrastructure* industry is one which provides an essential structure to enable other economic activities to exist. Without such structural bases, manufacturing industries in the old economy and intellectual property industries in the new economy could not function. They constitute the building blocks on which economic growth is created.

Companies providing the essential foundation for economic activity have historically experienced initial financial speculation due to excitement over investor prospects of high rates of return. Hype and promotion are used by brokerage firms to assist in the distribution of shares in companies with nominal sales and no earnings. And initially shares do rise, as investors hope for explosive growth in sales, earnings, and the price of their shares.

A period of disappointment typically follows, triggered by the realization that the market for the new products and services will require more time and capital to develop, and that many companies will fail. Investors may throw shares on the market in a frenzy of selling, or there may be an orderly market with slowly falling prices. Regardless, eventually there is a more realistic assessment of the long-term role of the industry's role as reflected in the stock prices of the constituent companies.

In the old economy, industrial progress required that a transportation system open access to markets outside of the cities, concurrently allowing farmers and ranchers to transport agriculture to large market centers. Other infrastructure industries included the electric and gas utilities for power; and the telephone and telegraph for communications. New economic infrastructure industries, discussed in this chapter, involve information and cash.

Depending on behavior and special characteristics, some infrastructure industries have been subject to government regulation and supervision. These include the railroads and truck transportation (the Interstate Commerce Commission or "ICC"), utilities (state public service commissions), the telephone system (the Federal Communications Commission or "FCC"), and banking (the Comptroller of the Currency). New economy industries of relatively recent invention have generally escaped such regulation, but are subject to antitrust and other legislation governing business activities.

However, this is a situation in flux. In the absence of new congressional action, the Clinton Administration actively restricted new economy industries in two notable situations.

- The U.S. Department of Justice's prosecution of Microsoft appears to signal that antitrust will remain national policy, and that monopolistic market control will not be allowed to develop.

- FTC approval of the AOL/Time Warner merger (see Chapter 6) involves oversight not previously imposed on similar mergers, including the appointment of a "monitor trustee" to oversee the company's competitive behavior.

However, there may be less strict enforcement in the incoming Bush Administration, and the final resolution is not clear.

An Old Economy Example: The Railroads

In the 19th century, agriculture was an industry in nearly pure competition, with many producers, no one of which could affect the price or the quantity offered. As such, sellers were essentially powerless to control their own destiny. When the railroads and manufacturing developed after the Civil War, their managers and investors were operating in largely unchartered economic waters.

In their ensuing scramble for market share, these new industrial sectors overbuilt, consumed vast amounts of capital, discounted prices to gain customers, frequently defaulted on their trade and debt obligations, and often failed. Before the creation of the Federal Reserve System in 1913, these events often led to general economic recession and widespread business failure.

A slowdown in construction in the railroad industry contributed to the panic of 1873, which lasted until the end of that decade. Further economic problems resulted from pauses in railroad activity, leading to a series of recessions in the 1890s. The industry recovered and continued its development, and the 20-year period before the First World War saw a huge expansion of passenger traffic and freight shipment. However, the intermittent boom/bust rail cycles caused widespread economic and social disruption.

A New Economy Example: Telecommunications

One of the glamour industries of the new economy has been telecommunications, led by global deregulation,[1] an array of new products and services, and superior earnings and stock market performance. But below the surface, it is an industry in turmoil, with competing technologies (i.e., wireline or wireless, narrowband or broadband), hundreds of new entrants, huge borrowing commitments and equity investments in capital assets, and fierce price competition. One estimate is that, in just the 1996 to 1999 period, $25 billion was raised through IPOs and another $82 billion in debt to construct communications networks, with total spending estimated in excess of $350 billion.[2]

Wall Street has become aware of the riskiness of this strategy, and telecom stock prices have plummeted, by more than 60% in the year 2000. Many investors have lost faith in the ability of the established companies (e.g., AT&T, certain of the Baby Bells) to compete, while finally realizing the precariousness of these high fixed investment business plans.

As this reevaluation occurs, the stock price and future of companies which supply equipment to the industry (i.e, Cisco Systems, Lucent, Copper Mountain, JDS Uniphase) are being affected. The inevitable result will be consolidation, failure, and reorganization until the economics of the industry rationalizes.[3]

Newer competitors, unencumbered by fixed asset commitments, are offering state-of-the-art technology to business and individual customers, such as fiber optics. It was expected that the breakthrough service and profit generator would be computer and Internet activity, and there is still the possibility that networks involving data, priority delivery, and other features can produce profits through value-added service.

What Investors Should Expect

The economic success/failure and stock price movement cycles of financial and information industries mimic the experiences of their late 19th and 20th century forerunners. One observer suggests that the new economy is comprised of two types of industries:

---

[1] U.S. deregulation in this industry resulted from the Telecommunications Act of 1996, Public Law 104-104, allowing new market entrants to offer local, long distance, and global telephone service.

[2] Stephanie N. Mehta, "Why Telecom Crashed," *Fortune Magazine*, November 27, 2000, pp. 125-129, at 127.

[3] For one set of predictions on the industry's future, see "Telecom's Wake-Up Call," *Business Week*, September 25, 2000, pp. 148-152.

- High capital cost industries, like the railroads, such as fixed fiber optics and cable communications, which are scrambling to capture market share to justify their initial investments.

- Innovative industries, like General Motors, such as personal computer manufacturers and financial service companies, which must continually develop new technology, develop new distribution channels, and add new product features.[4]

Moderate Success Inevitability

The apparent lesson in all of this is that once we were no longer primarily an agrarian society, boom-and-bust cycles in infrastructure industries became an inevitable outcome, given overinvestment, the scramble for customers, cutthroat competition, and success or failure. Lean and hungry entrepreneurs have the flexibility to respond to changing conditions, to attempt to achieve the return-on-investment expectations of investors, and to creatively destruct older businesses and grow newer, more competitive ones.

Companies with a major new economy image will likely retain that presence, with the inevitable entry of some new participants who eventually attain significant market share. Information and financial intermediaries with broad access to sources of supply and customers have a significant potential for long-term success.

The potential revenue stream for all participants could eventually be in the hundreds of millions of dollars. However, their successes will be moderate, not "home runs." The high tech stock market valuations of the second half of 1999 and early 2000 were never sustainable, and the subsequent collapse in stock prices could have been predicted.

Even when the various elements of the new economy infrastructure really get going, revenues to market participants will be limited by several factors.

- Transaction revenues will likely be based on competitive fees, not a percentage of the transaction amount. In this respect, companies providing information and cash infrastructure will operate in much the way that their predecessors have functioned. And the total fee revenue will not be enormous, given the experience of the telephone companies (e.g., long-distance at 5 cents a minute), banks (e.g., ACH electronic money transfers[5] at 10 cents per transaction), and railroads (e.g., interstate freight rates set by the ICC).

---

[4] Hal R. Varian, "Economic Scene," *The New York Times*, December 14, 2000, p. C2. See also, Michael Mandel, "Tech Leads — Both Up and Down," *Business Week*, December 18, 2000, pp. 62-63.

[5] ACH (Automated Clearing House) transactions are transmitted through a bank operated, money transfer system involving next-day funds settlement. ACHs are used for business transactions, including the movement of funds between banks, and for consumer transactions, such as direct deposit of payroll and the debiting of insurance premiums and mortgage payments.

- Direct selling firm-to-buying firm activity will constitute a significant volume of all infrastructure transactions. If General Motors chooses to deal directly with its suppliers, intermediaries will see zero revenue. Experience to the beginning of 2001 is limited, but the various advantages to private transactions — including preferred customer pricing, and quicker and more accurate service — suggest the likelihood of the majority of B2B through company-owned Websites.[6]

- Existing versions of infrastructure equipment, facilities, and software may be completely adequate for most business and consumer requirements. Unless there are important new innovations on existing technology, purchase decisions may well be deferred for years, severely hindering the flow of revenue, and threatening the existence of marginal providers.

The Moderate Winners: Information Industries

The moderate winners will be industries providing information and financial products and services to the companies to the big winners described in Chapter 6. This section discusses the information industries.

Computers and Office Equipment

There have been four elements in the strength of the computer and office equipment industry.

- Until 2000, personal computer shipments rose by 15% to 20% a year, driven by the need for business and personal Internet access, reductions in the cost of components, and general global economic prosperity.

- The server market should show continued growth through the support of Microsoft's Windows 2000 operating system for servers, which will compete with the dominant UNIX technology. (A client/server computer system allows a client — a personal computer — to request information services from a server — a larger, more powerful computer.)

- New products cause rapid computer obsolescence and support replacement sales. Non-legacy systems will be freed from the old PC look and can functionally integrate hardware and software, simplifying set-up and use. Appliance servers will provide dedicated tasks for information systems, such as managing a Website or operating a corporate ERP (enterprise resource planning) system.

---

[6] The early reports on B2B transaction activity indicate that this indeed may be the outcome. See, for example, "Let's Keep This Exchange to Ourselves," *Business Week*, December 4, 2000, p. 48.

- Direct selling through telephone and Websites has greatly reduced marketing costs while allowing manufacturers to control their distribution channels. Furthermore, buyers are paying for purchases prior to shipment or even product assembly, greatly reducing idle working capital.

However, sales growth rates are dropping as existing versions of PCs appear to satisfy most functions in general use and as penetration of the business market is nearly two-thirds of all U.S. workers and 85% of homes with high five-figure incomes.[7] The response of computer manufacturers has been to reduce prices in the hope of stimulating sales, and to integrate PCs with the newer peripheral devices.

Computer and office equipment companies ranked by revenue and growth in EPS are listed in Exhibit 7-1.

Computer Software, Services, and Peripherals

The $200 billion computer software, services, and peripherals industries continue to experience rapid life cycles. The likely moderate winners will be the larger, well capitalized companies with the capability to buy or compete with smaller firms offering innovative technologies.

Current interest is in several types of products:

- Integrative business systems, such as ERP, customer relationship management (CRM), supply-chain management (SCM), and integration software (which links discrete business systems)

- E-commerce systems for business-to-business applications (Ariba and numerous other vendors)

Exhibit 7-1: Computers and Office Equipment Companies

Companies Ranked by Revenue	Companies Ranked by EPS Growth
IBM	**Dell**
Hewlett-Packard	Sun Microsystems
Compaq	Hewlett-Packard
Dell	**Pitney Bowes**
Xerox	IBM
Sun Microsystems	**Silicon Graphics**
Gateway	**Compaq**
NCR	
Apple Computer	
Pitney Bowes	
Western Digital	
Silicon Graphics	

---

[7] Quentin Hardy, "Requiem for a Desktop," *Forbes Magazine*, January 8, 2001, pp. 56-57, citing International Data Corp., a marketing research firm.

Exhibit 7-2: Computer Software, Services and Peripherals

Companies Ranked by Revenue	Companies Ranked by EPS Growth
Microsoft	**Seagate Technology**
EDS	Microsoft
Oracle	BMC Software
Computer Sciences	**Oracle**
Unisys	American Management Systems
Seagate Technology	Fiserv
EMC	Equifax
ADP	**Computer Associates**
First Data	**Computer Sciences**
Science Applications Intl.	**ADP**
Computer Associates	Novell

NOTE: Several leading companies in the Computer Software, Services, and Peripherals businesses are excluded because they have not been in existence as public companies for the entire 1989-1999 period; e.g., Peoplesoft, Quantum, and EDS.

- Upgrades and new versions of operating and support systems, such as Windows 2000 (Microsoft) and Netware 5.0 (Novell); antivirus software (Network Associates/McAfee and Norton/Symantec); and security software (VeriSign and Check Point)

- Outsourcing (applicable to both computer equipment and software) by the largest technology companies for cost reduction, to accelerate development time, and to avoid owning equipment which becomes rapidly obsolete, to such firms as EDS, Computer Sciences, IBM, and Accenture (formerly Andersen Consulting); for disaster recovery services (Comdisco and SunGard); and for payroll (ADP and Ceridian)

- Software and peripherals for new consumer products, such as handheld computers, music players, digital cameras, and business-to-consumer Internet systems

Other maturing products have entered lagging cycles, including standard mainframe and personal computer software, due to lackluster equipment sales and the apparent end of Y2K problems.

Computer software, services and peripheral companies ranked by revenue and growth in EPS are listed in Exhibit 7-2.

Network Communications and Telecommunications

When the Federal Communications allowed competitive operating companies into local telephone service (beginning in the New York City metropolitan area), the telecommunications industry entered a new era of competition. With the various component segments vying for wireless, Internet, local, and long distance services, there will be a long period of consolidation, price cutting, and the realignment of traditional market definitions. Mergers recently completed include WorldCom/MCI (1998), Vodafone AirTouch/Mannesmann (1999 and 2000), Time Warner/GST Telecommunications (2000), and Verizon/Nortpoint Communications (2000).

The industry will redefine its basic revenue sources, focusing on enhanced services such as Web hosting, wireless data services, and Internet access, including short text messages. Long distance and some local telephone service will be offered at low cost (or free) to gain users of for-fee services (such as the Internet). To support all of this bandwidth demand, telecommunication equipment companies will be expanding, raising new capital, and acquiring competitors, such as Nortel's purchase of Qtera (2000).

Network communications and telecommunications companies ranked by revenue and growth in EPS are listed in Exhibit 7-3.

Semiconductors

Chipmakers have enjoyed decades of success due to demand for semiconductors, microprocessors, communications, industrial equipment, the military, networking services, new entertainment products (e.g., high resolution television, DVD players, cameras), and communications products. The development of new devices for Internet access will drive sales for production equipment and for new generations of chip technology.

Although subject to the general economic cycle and some periods of overcapacity, the industry continues to sell in excess of $20 billion of product worldwide. The chip manufacturing process has become increasingly complex due primarily to miniaturization, causing market share to migrate toward larger companies capable of affording new process technology. The trend continues of increased functionality, speed and memory capacity, with ever declining prices (as predicted by Moore's Law).

Exhibit 7-3: Network Communications and Telecommunications

Companies Ranked by Revenue	Companies Ranked by EPS Growth
AT&T	**MCI Worldcom**
SBC	Tellabs
Lucent Technologies	Telephone & Data Systems
MCI Worldcom	Centurytel
Bell Atlantic	3Com
GTE	ADC Telecommunications
BellSouth	SBC
Sprint	Alltel
US West	**GTE**
Cisco Systems	**Bellsouth**
	Bell Atlantic

Exhibit 7-4: Semiconductors

Companies Ranked by Revenue	Companies Ranked by EPS Growth
Intel	Intel
Texas Instruments	**Analog Devices**
Advanced Micro Devices	**Texas Instruments**
LSI Logic	
National Semiconductor	
Amkor Technology	
Analog Devices	

Note: LSI Logic and Amkor Technology do not have a 10-year earnings record.

Recent price cutting by Intel and Advanced Micro Devices is not likely to continue with the continuing demand for chips, and the earnings of these companies and their smaller rivals should recover in the long term. Strong demand in this industrial sector will come for the products that run business computing: workstations, computer servers, PCs, and laptops, particularly in the emerging transition to e-commerce.

Semiconductor companies ranked by revenue and growth in EPS are listed in Exhibit 7-4.

Publishing and Advertising

Many observers thought that the publishing industry was becoming a dinosaur when Internet services became widely available and threatened readership and advertising revenue. However, there has been an escalation in advertising from the new media as heroic efforts are being made to capture name recognition. The penetration success of the Internet is impressive, but cannot compare with television and radio ownership (in more than 98% of U.S. households); newspaper readership (about 125 million daily readers); or magazine circulation (about 350 million copies each month).

The print and broadcast media are driven by advertising and cannot survive on subscription and newsstand revenue. The robust economy provided a strong incentive to use this form of marketing, and a softening may seriously impact certain marginal publications. Advertising revenue is also affected by the trend toward local promotions, such as sports and music events, led by Anheuser-Busch (Budweiser beer) and Ford Motor.

Consolidation will likely continue to increase market share and reduce costs. Recent publishing mergers involved large European publishers. Significant U.S. transactions include Conde Nast/Fairchild (1999), Tele-Communications/TV Guide (1998), American Media/Evercore Capital Partners (1999), and various book publisher deals. However, publishing remains a very fragmented industry, involving tens of thousands of firms which face labor-intensive processes; a scramble for finite advertising budgets; and paper, production and distribution costs.

Publishers and advertising firms ranked by revenue and growth in EPS are listed in Exhibit 7-5.

Exhibit 7-5: Publishing and Advertising

Companies Ranked by Revenue	Companies Ranked by EPS Growth
R.R. Donnelly & Sons	**McGraw-Hill**
Gannett	**Tribune Co.**
Omnicom Group	A.H. Belo
Interpublic Group	Reynolds & Reynolds
McGraw-Hill	Omnicom Group
Knight-Ridder	American Greetings
Tribune Co.	**Interpublic Group**
Times Mirror	Gannett
New York Times	Wallace
Reader's Digest	Standard Register

The Moderate Winners: Industries Which Manage Cash

This section discusses the financial industries, including banking, diversified financials, and insurance.

Banking

Banks are institutions which take deposits and make loans, earning a spread on the difference between the cost of funds, the interest paid on deposits or on inter-bank financings (in the federal funds market), and the interest received on loans and from other fee income. Earnings from traditional business credit have recently been declining as banks are deemphasizing lending, forcing borrowers to seek other financing sources. For those loans outstanding, there is widespread concern for credit quality in softening economic conditions, particularly as lenders have been lax in applying appropriate stress tests to determine if borrowers can repay in a period of economic shocks.

Banks are aggressively managing both the revenue and expense portions of their income statements. On the revenue side, some bank income has been replaced through the sale of non-credit commercial services, such as cash management, custody, trust services, trade finance and foreign exchange, and through such consumer activities as mortgage and personal lending, and credit cards.

On the cost side, the ending of McFadden Act (interstate banking) and Glass-Stegall Act (the mingling of investment and commercial banking) restrictions has enabled significant consolidation in the industry. This permits the lowering of such non-interest costs as staff, systems, and physical facilities, with the number of banks declining by more than one-third in the past two decades. Other expense initiatives include:

- reducing teller staffing through increased use of ATMs

- efforts to promote commercial and consumer banking through the Internet

- the use of established distribution channels in diversified financial companies and securities firms through mergers or alliances

- securitizing packages of receivables (i.e., mortgages) for sale as public market debt instruments, allowing the removal of the receivable from the books of the bank

Commercial banks ranked by revenue and growth in EPS are listed in Exhibit 7-6.

Diversified Financials and Securities Firms

Diversified financial companies are similar to banks, in that many take deposits or investments and finance business or consumer transactions. Some important differences are that the industry is generally less regulated, offers products to specific market segments, supports the transaction of a related business[8] resulting in lower marketing costs, and realizes fairly wide spreads over the cost of funds (averaging 7% to 10% for consumer financing).

A significant marketing development in the past decade has been the use of credit cards for nearly any type of purchase by all economic strata. The potential profitability of cards has led to various innovations, including affinity cards, providing a tie-in with a favorite business or not-for-profit organization; and purchasing cards, simplifying the procurement of small items by businesses.

However, a slowing economy will negatively impact any credit card debt as credit quality deteriorates and repayments are jeopardized. This concern is intensified by the ease of filing for bankruptcy; increasing rates of divorce, often eliminating the second person responsible for the debt; and a general lack of consumer financial prudence and knowledge.

Exhibit 7-6: Banking

Companies Ranked by Revenue	Companies Ranked by EPS Growth
Bank of America	**Bank of New York**
Chase Manhattan/J.P. Morgan	First Tennessee
Bank One	Zions Bancorp
First Union	M&T Bank Corp.
Wells Fargo	State Street Corp.
FleetBoston	Synovus Financial
U.S. Bancorp	Comerica
National City Corp.	Fifth Third Bancorp
Keycorp	Firstar Corp.
PNC Financial	**Wells Fargo**
Suntrust Banks	Northern Trust
Bank of New York	Compass Bancshares

[8] Examples include home purchases, automobiles, professional and office equipment, and consumer leisure and recreation.

Exhibit 7-7: Diversified Financials and Securities Firms

Companies Ranked by Revenue	Companies Ranked by EPS Growth
General Electric	**Paine Webber Group**
Citigroup/Associates 1st Captl.	Countrywide Credit
Fannie Mae	Citigroup/Associates 1st Captl.
Freddie Mac	**Washington Mutual**
American Express	Fidelity National Financial
Washington Mutual	**Freddie Mac**
Household International	Franklin Resources
Marsh & McLennan	**Fannie Mae**
Bear Stearns	**Bear Stearns**
Paine Webber Group	SLM Holding

NOTE: The four largest securities firm, Merrill Lynch, Morgan Stanley Dean Witter, Goldman Sachs Group, and Lehman Bros. Holdings are excluded as they have not been public companies for the entire 1989-1999 period

There have been several strategic developments in the securities brokerage industry in the past decade. These include:

- the movement to shorter clearing and settlement times

- the migration to nearly universal book-entry transaction crediting

- the rise of the on-line, discount brokerage concept

- public ownership of firms previously managed as partnerships (i.e., Goldman Sachs) and the merger of others into commercial banks (i.e., Bank of America's 1997 acquisition of Montgomery Securities)

- the globalization of financial markets

- the rising demand for investment products by baby-boomers preparing for retirement

The industry's capital requirements, increasing profit pressures, and the need for expanded distribution channels will inevitably drive further merger activity with other financial industry companies.

Diversified financial companies and securities firms ranked by revenue and growth in EPS are listed in Exhibit 7-7.

Insurance

The insurance industry has experienced years of mediocre growth, a general lack of buyer interest in traditional insurance and investment products, competitive pressure, customer resistance to property insurance premium increases, and significant underwriting losses. Regulatory restrictions had prevented incursions into banking and brokerage products, and the mutual form of ownership characteristic of about half of all insurers prevents the raising of equity capital for acquisition or other new ventures. Companies recently choosing to demutualize include Prudential (approved in late 2000 for implementation in 2001), John Hancock (2000), Met Life (2000), and Mutual of New York (1998).

The consolidation in this industry, previously involving insurance companies in similar businesses (i.e., Mass Mutual and Connecticut Mutual), will follow the lead of the more diversified Citigroup (Citicorp/Travelers) merger (1998). However, these may be difficult deals to strike, given the lagging return-on-equities of insurance companies (averaging 9%) to those of banks (18%), diversified financials (16%), and securities firms (20%).[9] Other than sheer size and market penetration, the most attractive feature of the insurance business may be the popularity of hybrid investment-insurance products, such as variable annuities.

Variable annuities have particular appeal for baby boomers needing retirement funds to supplement their expected Social Security and pension incomes. These products now sell in excess of $100 billion annually, driven by the attraction of tax-free exchanges into different investment options and the combination of stock market returns with traditional insurance protection. However, sales charges are high, and competition may reduce profitability while the recent market downturn affects likely new sales.

Insurance companies ranked by revenue and growth in EPS are listed in Exhibit 7-8.

Information and Financial Infrastructure Companies

Within the infrastructure industries, the companies which meet our criteria include 18 providing information services and 7 offering cash and financial services.

Exhibit 7-8: Insurance[a]

Companies Ranked by Revenue	Companies Ranked by EPS Growth
AIG	**AFLAC**
Allstate	Conseco
Met Life	Protective Life
Berkshire Hathaway[b]	Jefferson-Pilot
Loews	Progressive
Hartford Financial Services	Mercury General
American General	AIG
UnumProvident	American National Insurance
St. Paul Companies	Reliastar Financial
AFLAC	Berkshire Hathaway[b]

[a] Does not include mutual ownership companies
[b] Excluded as stock trades in the range of $55-$65,000 per share

---

[9] The weighted average ROE for the insurance companies reported in *Fortune* categories 29-32, including life and health mutual and stock companies, and property and casualty mutual and stock companies. ROEs reported directly include: banks, industry no. 9; diversified financials, no. 14; and securities firms, no. 49. "Fortune 500 Issue," *Fortune Magazine*, April 17, 2000, pp. F-57 to F-72.

Information Services

Company/ Symbol/Beta	Industry	Sales (millions)	Principal Company Businesses
Compaq Computer (CPQ)/1.25	Computers and Office equipment	$38,525.0 (FY 1999)	Computer systems, including hardware and software, servers and technology services
Dell (DELL)/1.30	Computers and Office Equipment	$25,265.0 (FY 2000)	Computer systems, including desktop, notebook and enterprise systems (includes servers and workstations)
Pitney Bowes (PBI)/1.00	Computers and Office Equipment	$4,432.6 (FY 1999)	Postage meters, mailing equipment and fax machines; shipping and weighing systems; sales financing of office equipment; online and Internet-based services
SCI Systems (SCI)/1.75	Computers and Office Equipment	$6,710.8 (FY 1999)	Products and services for the computer, telecommunications, medical, industrial, consumer, military and aerospace industries
Silicon Graphics (SGI)/1.30	Computers and Office Equipment	$2,331.1 (FY 2000)	High-end servers; graphics computers for movie special effects; modeling and animation software; microprocessors
Sun Microsystems (SUNW)/1.25	Computers and Office Equipment	$15,721.0 (FY 2000)	UNIX-based workstation computers, storage devices, and servers for computer networks and Web sites; Java, a "universal" programming language
ADP (ADP)/0.75	Software and Peripherals	$6,287.5 (FY 2000)	Payroll, human resources, benefits administration, time and attendance, and tax filing and reporting; brokerage, auto dealer, and insurance claim services
Computer Associates (CA)/1.60	Software and Peripherals	$6,103.0 (FY 2000)	Design, development, sales and supports for integrated computer software products and network management tools
Computer Sciences (CSC)/0.90	Software and Peripherals	$9,371.0 (FY 2000)	Information technology services through outsourcing; systems integration; and IT and management consulting services
Oracle (ORCL)/1.70	Software and Peripherals	$10,130.0 (FY 2000)	Database management systems software; develops and distributes systems and business applications software
Verizon (VZ)/0.65	Network Communications and Telecommunications	$33,174 (FY 1999)	Leading provider of high-growth communication services formed from Bell Atlantic and GTE; #1 local phone company/#2 telecom services provider with 63 million local-access lines in 31 states
Bellsouth (BLS)/0.50	Network Communications and Telecommunications	$25,224 (FY 1999)	Wireline services for voice, digital and data, cable and digital TV, and wireless communications in 20 countries; local phone service in 9 Southeastern states
Worldcom (WCOM)/1.55	Network Communications and Telecommunications	$37,120 (FY 1999)	Global communications and managed network services; local service in more than 20 countries; data services to businesses over an Internet backbone

Company/ Symbol/Beta	Industry	Sales (millions)	Principal Company Businesses
Analog Devices (ADI)/2.25	Semiconductors	$2,578.0 (FY 2000)	Precision analog, mixed-signal and digital signal integrated circuits used in processing applications
Texas Instruments (TXN)/1.70	Semiconductors	$9,468 (FY 1999)	Manufacturer of analog and logic chips, microprocessors, microcontrollers and digital signal processing systems
Interpublic Group (IPG)/1.00	Publishing and Advertising	$4,427.3 (FY 1999)	Advertising agencies and marketing service companies for more than 4,000 clients including Internet, marketing, and public relations services
McGraw-Hill (MHP)/0.85	Publishing and Advertising	$3,992.0 (FY 1999)	Publishing and information including books, magazines, newsletters, software, on-line services, CD-ROMs, TV and textbooks
Tribune Co. (TRB)/0.60	Publishing and Advertising	$3,221.9 (FY 1999)	Newspapers, books, educational materials, and broadcasting and distributing information and entertainment

Financial Services

Company/ Symbol/Beta	Industry	Sales (millions)	Principal Company Businesses
Bank of New York (BK)/1.30	Banking	$6,966.0 (FY 1999)	Commercial and consumer loans; residential mortgages; securities and processing; investment banking; trust, investment management, private and retail banking
Wells Fargo (WFC)/1.00	Banking	$21,795.0 (FY 1999)	Consumer and business banking services; investment services and products; real estate and consumer loans; international trade; Internet banking
Bear Stearns (BSC)/1.75	Diversified Financial	$7,882.0 (FY 1999)	Investment banking, securities trading, asset management and brokerage services for corporations, governments, institutional and individual investors
Fannie Mae (FNM)/0.60	Diversified Financial	$36,968.0 (FY 1999)	Financial products and services providing liquidity in the mortgage market by buying mortgages from lenders which are securitized for resale
Freddie Mac (FRE)/0.80	Diversified Financial	$24,268.0 (FY 1999)	Functions like Fannie Mae but also retains some mortgages as investments
Washington Mutual (WM)/0.90	Diversified Financial	$13,571.0 (FY 1999)	Regional financial services including traditional consumer and commercial banking for consumers and mid-sized businesses
AFLAC (AFL)/1.10	Insurance	$8,640.0 (FY 1999)	Supplemental medical insurance policies for U.S. and Japanese markets for special conditions, (e.g., cancer, and intensive and long-term care)

FINAL THOUGHTS ABOUT THE MODERATE WINNERS

We have listed 25 companies providing essential infrastructure to the "big" winners. These companies demonstrated an interesting mix of aggressive growth (the information providers) and staid performance (the financial organizations) until the stock market downturn in 2000 challenged perceptions of value and risk-return. They will continue to show decent returns over the long term, and should be included in most portfolios. However, "moderate" winner returns will not be exceptional, certainly nothing like the results that will be accomplished by the "big" winners.

Chapter 8

The Losers

You don't need an M.B.A. from Harvard to figure out how to lose money.
Royal Little, *1896-1989 (founder of Textron, the first U.S. conglomerate)*

We've looked at the big winners and the moderate winners. This chapter looks at the losers — the industries which will not be willing or able to take advantage of the changes caused by the e-commerce, new economy, and will continue to try to compete using 20th century rules. Their managements do not or cannot continuously innovate, respond to changing conditions, or redefine their business strategy. Rather, they rest on past accomplishments, or struggle to survive in a highly competitive environment.

We cannot know which companies will leap to a dominant position in their industries, or which will decline from a previously commanding role. The difficulty for management and for the investor is in envisioning the next market, emerging technology or competitive challenge to renew the growth cycle. All we can do is to consider whether the economic structure of an industry is supportive of investment success or mediocrity.

FACTORS SUGGESTING FAILURE

There are four underlying reasons for the categorization of industries or specific companies as investment "losers".

- *Dispersion.* The industry is dispersed and is unlikely to become concentrated due to economic or structural factors.

- *Size.* The leading companies in an industry are too big to adjust to changing competitive conditions, to adapt new technology, or to respond to customer demands for product innovation.

- *Basic Industry.* The goods and services provided are basic and do not involve production processes which significantly alter the essential structure of the materials used.

- *Deregulation.* The industry is emerging from regulation and the outcome in general and for specific companies is uncertain.

These factors are discussed in the sections which follow.[1] Although we consider them as "loser" industries, prominent companies are listed in the format used in Chapters 6 and 7, showing revenue and growth in EPS. The purpose is to provide data on stocks you may currently hold or are considering. Our review is primarily for purposes of illustrating each "loser" type, and is not intended to be exhaustive.

Exceptional Companies

While this chapter deals with "losers," any particular company may excel and show outstanding results within these industries. Examples we previously cited were Wal-Mart in consumer retailing and Enron in energy distribution. Such superior performance is often a result of the corporate culture of the CEO, as at Enron, which may be instilled and perpetuated by a founder, as at Wal-Mart.

The market price of Enron and Wal-Mart shares (and other superior companies in "loser" industries) reflect these results, and the investor should not assume that tomorrow's performance by future leadership will match current successes. In fact, our experience with cycles of growth, stagnation and decline, as previously described, suggests that such performance may not be sustainable in the long run.

DISPERSED AND UNLIKELY TO CONCENTRATE

Dispersion occurs when economies of scale, technology or other barriers to entry are not significant. Exhibit 5-3 provided a list of representative industries, indicating that the value added by the eight largest companies is only 40%. In other words, any company with a reasonable amount of capital and expertise can enter or exit the industry at almost any time. Industries in this situation are poor candidates for transition to the e-commerce, new economy.

The continuing struggle to survive — while competing with other companies — requires the commitment of most of their available human and financial capital. We discuss three sectors: retailing and wholesaling, food products, and industrial machinery and equipment. Other industries not specifically discussed include apparel and textiles, furniture, and real estate.

Retailing and Wholesaling

Retailing and wholesaling will not experience any significant benefit from the new economy other than in the procurement process for inventory. While it will be attractive for large retailers to be able to order on-line as product trends are perceived, the major cost elements in the distribution sector will not be significantly affected: labor costs in warehousing, in buying, and on the retail floor; site costs; marketing; and customer service including credit and returns.

---

[1] Some of these issues were first introduced in Chapter 5.

Exhibit 8-1: Retailing and Wholesaling

Companies Ranked by Revenue	Companies Ranked by EPS Growth
Wal-Mart	Best Buy
Sears Roebuck	Tech Data
Home Depot	Safeguard Scientifics
KMart	Dollar General
Target	Home Depot
J.C. Penney	Anixter Intl.
McKesson HBOC	Gap
Ingram Micro	Saks
Costco	Office Depot
Cardinal Health	Owens & Minor
Federated Dept. Stores	Watsco
Sysco	Lowe's

On-line retailing volume will continue at nominal volumes relative to total retail sales, certainly less than 5%, and will not be a major factor in increasing retail volume overall. The consumer must continue to spend for retailing to succeed as an investment, as evidenced by the weak Christmas season of 2000. In fact, the dispersion of the retail industry has caused significant overcapacity, with specialty retail space up about 20% since 1998.

Wholesaling has become fragmented and organized generally by industry specialization, and is most likely to gain from e-commerce by supply management efficiencies. The major companies service the construction industries for materials, equipment, and supplies (e.g., Hughes Supply and Fastenal) and for healthcare services for hospitals, pharmacies, physicians and long-term care (e.g., McKesson HBOC).

Retailers and wholesalers ranked by revenue and growth in EPS are listed in Exhibit 8-1.

Food Distribution and Services

The biggest single impact on food distribution and services is the economy. In prosperity, people tend to eat at restaurants or order take-out, and consequently do less home preparation. The result is a nearly $400 billion restaurant industry in the United States. As the economy softens, the supermarket and food manufacturing sectors should improve from their recent nominal growth rates.

Consolidation will continue in all food sectors to reduce costs and improve distribution. Recent mergers included Kellogg/Keebler (2001), Unilever/Bestfoods (2000), Pepsi/Quaker Oats (2000), and several acquisitions by the retailers Kroger and Albertson's. Companies will be selling underperforming businesses, reducing the number of branded products, and managing costs to compete with the newest major food retailer, Wal-Mart.

E-commerce is primarily being applied in the improved utilization of food transport and in inventory management. Although these opportunities are significant, the dispersion of the industry and limited opportunity for revenue growth does not warrant inclusion in your investment strategy.

Food companies ranked by revenue and growth in EPS are listed in Exhibit 8-2.

Industrial Machinery and Equipment

Industrial machinery and equipment consists of agricultural, construction and transportation equipment; industrial machinery; and engineering and construction services. Of all of the loser industries, the capital goods sector probably has the greatest opportunity to become a winner. In fact, transportation and equipment appears as a "big winner" in the discussion in Chapter 6. However, the historic dispersion among the other capital goods industries results in their "loser" categorization.

The close correlation with general economic conditions, now clearly becoming weak, does not portend a positive outlook in the near future. The current emphasis is on cost reduction, manufacturing simplification, and the integration/replacement of electronics in mechanical systems, and e-commerce will be used to reduce inventories by direct ordering, customization, and changes in product design.

Manufacturers will continue to seek new sales in global markets, assisting in the development of power, transportation, and agricultural infrastructure. However, U.S. companies face issues of sovereign (country) risk, weak developing economies, and favoritism to local (and often inept) companies.

Companies manufacturing industrial machinery and equipment are listed in Exhibit 8-3, ranked by revenue and growth in EPS.

TOO BIG TO ADJUST

In nearly every industry, the largest companies are like the proverbial battleship: nearly impossible to turn and face a nimble, vigorous enemy. These companies are simply too unwieldy to adjust to respond to competitive actions, cannot quickly implement the latest technology, or do not appreciate that the market demands constant innovation.

Exhibit 8-2: Food Distribution and Services

Companies Ranked by Revenue	Companies Ranked by EPS Growth
Kroger	Campbell Soup
Albertson's	CBRL Group
Safeway	Brinker Intl.
CVS	Wendy's Intl.
Walgreen	Publix
Winn-Dixie Stores	Walgreen
McDonald's	McDonald's
Publix	Hannaford Bros.
Rite Aid	Ruddick
Nebco Evans	Winn-Dixie Stores
Tricon Global	Albertson's

Exhibit 8-3: Industrial Machinery and Equipment

Companies Ranked by Revenue	Companies Ranked by EPS Growth
Caterpillar	Dover
Halliburton	Black & Decker
Fluor	Clayton Homes
Deere	Toll Brothers
Ingersoll-Rand	Centex
American Standard	Jacobs Engineering
Cummins Engine	Pulte
Centex	Terex
Parker Hannifin	Teleflex
Baker Hughes	Lennar
ITT Industries	Ingersoll-Rand
Black & Decker	Milacron
Dover	Parker Hannifin

It is typical for very large, dominant companies to experience cycles of growth, stagnation, and decline. Some examples in the recent past:

- The computer industry — now a half century old — whose products have been commercially available since IBM introduced the 1400 series in the 1950s and the 360 series in the 1960s. IBM dominated the computer mainframe industry through the 1980s, only to see its market position eroded by the rise of the personal computer and the explosive growth of software companies. Competitors continual development of new systems, applications, and connectivity nearly destroyed IBM, until new management realigned priorities and reorganized to meet customer needs.[2]

- DuPont has failed to aggressively respond to changing market conditions, relying on such older products as basic chemicals, synthetic fibers, and herbicide. These businesses have become only marginally profitable, while competitors developed integrated product groupings fostered by extensive investment in research.

The following sections describe a prominent "too big to adjust" industry: automobile manufacturing.

Automobiles — Early 20th Century

Ford and General Motors were industry leaders, then became complacent and lost their dominant positions to global competitors. In the five year 1904 to 1908 period, 240 companies entered the automobile business. By 1910, an economic recession had closed many of these companies. Henry Ford then organized the industry's modern industrial form through mass production and vertical integration. Automobile manu-

---

[2] See Daniel Q. Mills and G. Bruce Friesen, *Broken Promises*, Harvard Business School Press, 1996; and Emerson W. Pugh, *Building IBM*, MIT Press, 1995.

facturing was originally a highly fragmented business, comprised of craftsmen from such collateral industries as bicycle and carriage manufacturing. Ford's ability to greatly reduce the cost to manufacture transformed this situation to one of oligopoly.

As the industry leader — Ford produced almost one-half of the cars sold in the United States by 1923 — the company seized market share and drove small competitors out of business. Ford Motor owned raw materials sources, controlled the conversion to finished goods, managed distribution process to the ultimate consumer, and partnered with tire and other suppliers to assure a constant flow of quality components. However, customers were eventually put off by limited styles, forms, and colors,[3] and Ford was eventually displaced as industry leader by General Motors, which changed the marketing "hook" from pricing to product differentiation.

Automobiles: The Current Situation

Today's General Motors has experienced a steady decline in market share. The Oldsmobile Division, a successor to a company founded in 1897, has been slated for closure. Olds sold more than a million units a year until the 1970s. However, the impact of competition from imports and the general impression of stodginess eventually caused the loss of significant numbers of formerly loyal customers.

Ford Motor remains as the other major American competitor to GM. To some extent, Ford's current problems have resulted from the actions of others: the Bridgestone-Firestone tire shredding problem;[4] and the global oversupply of vehicles, resulting in short-term price cuts, no interest financing, and the prospect of some permanent plant closings. Ford experienced a negative total return to investors in 1999 even though reported profits led the industry, indicating that investor expectations are pessimistic. You should be too.

A major third competitor, DaimlerChrysler (1998), was created to merge a luxury car line (Mercedes Benz) with the more moderately priced vehicles sold by Chrysler. However, cultural differences between the nationalities involved (Americans and Germans) have been difficult to overcome, finally resulting in the decision in 1999 to operate Chrysler and Mercedes as independent businesses. This foregoes much of the cost and managerial synergies originally expected from the merger.

Automobile manufacturers ranked by revenue and growth in EPS are listed in Exhibit 8-4.

Exhibit 8-4: Automobile Manufacturing

Companies Ranked by Revenue	Companies Ranked by EPS Growth
General Motors	DaimlerChrysler[a]
Ford Motor	General Motors
DaimlerChrysler	Ford Motor

[a] 10-year EPS not available; ranking represents 3-year results.

[3] Henry Ford's famous quote was: "Any customer can have a car painted any color that he wants so long as it is black." Statement to Plant Superintendent Charles Sorensen in 1912. Cited in Allan Nevins, *Ford*, Columbia University and Ford Motor Company (1954), p. 452.

[4] See Chapter 7.

Exhibit 8-5: Basic Industries

SIC Description and Number Reference	Shipments/Receipts ($MM)	% Value Added By 8 Largest Companies
Agribusiness (207, 213, 214)	$17,212	92
Petroleum and Coal (2911)	$136,579	49
Stone, Clay & Glass (32)	$38,777	42
Primary Metals (33)	$106,538	54
Total Basic Industries	$299,106	52

The largest sectors are included, those where annual sales exceed $10 billion.

Source: See Exhibit 5-3, footnote b.

BASIC INDUSTRIES

We previously noted that basic industries primarily function to convert raw materials to a more finished form, as in the cracking of petroleum to make refined oil products. Exhibit 8-5, which lists selected basic industries, shows that the average value added by the largest companies is about 50% (although it exceeds 90% for the three SICs included in the agribusiness sector).

Like many old economy industries, companies in these industries will continue to provide critically needed materiel to the global marketplace. However, the most significant opportunity for basic industries from the new economy will be in the application of sophisticated technology for inventory management and distribution. The industries in this situation include building materials, glass, waste management, energy, agribusiness, and metals. We'll review the latter three sectors.

Energy

The energy industry complex includes oil, gas, coal, and petroleum services, and all are affected by a variety of exogenous factors: OPEC and non-OPEC producer decisions on the amount of oil to bring to market; changes in U.S. political and regulatory positions (e.g., whether to use the strategic reserve inventory in times of tight supply, whether to drill in environmentally protected areas); the strength of the world economy; and various global geopolitical issues.

Energy tends to experience demand/supply cycles: demand is driven by weather, economic activity, or political crisis; investment follows in new exploration and drilling/mining; and finally excess supply drives prices lower. The situation at the beginning of 2001 appears to reflect a gradual move toward equilibrium after a period of rising prices and increased exploration, possibly leading to reduced profitability for many participants. The excess of OPEC supply may be some two million barrels per day, the number of working rigs is 40% higher than three years ago,[5] and natural gas exploration has increased significantly.

---

[5] Estimate by Deutsche Banc Alex. Brown, in "Energy," special "Industry Outlook" survey, *Business Week*, January 8, 2001, p. 122.

Exhibit 8-6: Energy

Companies Ranked by Revenue	Companies Ranked by EPS Growth
Exxon Mobil	Chevron
Enron	MidAmerica Energy Hldgs.
Texaco	Tosco
Chevron	Phillips Petroleum
USX	Coastal
Conoco	Ashland
Dynegy	Apache
Tosco	Williams
Phillips Petroleum	Enron
Atlantic Richfield	Murphy Oil
Ult. Diamond Shamrock	
El Paso Energy	

Costs and refinery capacity have been reduced in recent years through industry consolidation, including the BP/Amoco (1998) and Exxon/Mobil (1999) mergers. Future deals are likely to involve smaller independents given antitrust concerns both in the United States and Europe. Technologies to reduce costs include horizontal drilling to minimize the sinking of multiple wells per reservoir and increase recovery; measurement while drilling, allowing real-time geological evaluation; and 3-D seismic analysis of site acoustics. E-commerce is not yet an important factor in the cost structure of the energy complex.

Energy companies ranked by revenue and growth in EPS are listed in Exhibit 8-6.

Agribusiness

The modern agriculture/agribusiness and food processing industries apply business methodology and large capital investments to replace the family farm. Like the other basic industries, financial results are subject to various factors beyond the direct control of the companies, including weather and growing conditions, global demand, government subsidies, the general economy, and consumer reactions to food safety, including genetic modification and food diseases.

There may be further industry consolidation in the current cost management environment driven by oversupply, weak commodity prices, and a soft global economy. The year 2001 began with a merger between Tyson/IBP. Previously, Monsanto (now part of Pharmacia & Upjohn) bought DEKALB (1998), and DuPont acquired Pioneer Hi-Bred (1998).

E-commerce will not be an important element in agribusiness, although there will some efforts toward improving sales, distribution, and inventory management through Internet initiatives. A major impact of e-commerce will be in agricultural biotechnology, intended to extend shelf life, improve crop yields, resist pests, and enhance nutrition, through information exchange on optimal combinations of seed, fertilizer, pesticide, and crop rotation. However, the future of genetic engineering is uncertain, given consumer resistance to altered foods and concern over food diseases.

Exhibit 8-7: Agribusiness

Companies Ranked by Revenue	Companies Ranked by EPS Growth
Conagra	H.J. Heinz
Sara Lee	IBP
Archer Daniels Midland	Smithfield Foods
IBP	Hershey Foods
H.J. Heinz	Wm. Wrigley
Bestfoods	Sara Lee
Nabisco Group	Pilgrim's Pride
Tyson Foods	Quaker Oats
Kellogg	Dean Foods
Campbell Soup	Hormel Foods
General Mills	Bestfoods
Dole Foods	

Note: Farmland Industries is excluded as it is a farmer-owned cooperative

Exhibit 8-8: Metals

Companies Ranked by Revenue	Companies Ranked by EPS Growth
Alcoa	Nucor
Reynolds Metals	Commercial Metals
AK Steel Holding	Alcoa
LTV	
Nucor	
Bethlehem Steel	
Allegheny Technologies	
Phelps Dodge	

Agribusinesses ranked by revenue and growth in EPS are listed in Exhibit 8-7.

Metals

The steel industry was a giant in the first half of the 20th century, producing the essential component for construction, automobiles, defense, and numerous other uses. Integrated steel production required enormous capital investment, precluding the entry of new competitors and assuring oligopolistic control of pricing and supply for such leading companies as U.S. Steel (now USX) and Bethlehem Steel. However, the introduction in the last 20 years of the minimill and thin slab casting has allowed a global industry to develop, causing severe price competition and mediocre profits.

The production of aluminum continues to require significant economies of scale and remains as a concentrated industry, with about a dozen participants. Both metals, as well as copper, lead, zinc, and nickel, have been adversely affected by overcapacity; the substitution by such other materials as plastics, glass, and ceramics; and the softening global economy. For the metals industry reported in the Fortune 500 list (category 36), the 10-year growth in EPS is −2%.

Metals companies ranked by revenue and growth in EPS are listed in Exhibit 8-8.

DEREGULATION

Deregulation was previously noted as an important factor in the development of emerging oligopolies in several industries. Federal and state regulation of specific markets first developed in response to near monopoly control and predatory behavior by the leading companies.[6] Over time, it gradually became apparent that the very process of regulation stifled innovation and growth, while guaranteeing a reasonable rate of return even to inefficient organizations.

The deregulation of the airline industry, effectuated by the ending the control of pricing and route structure by the Civil Aeronautics Board beginning in 1978, began a steady evolution away from governmental control. Industries evolving from a regulated status suddenly face competitive pressures not previously experienced.

- Utilities are no longer restricted by geographic boundaries, and several are expanding into global businesses.

- The airlines enter and leave markets, charge market prices for seats, and behave as any other competitive industry.

- Banks and stock brokers are entering each other's markets, and various mergers have occurred involving these industries.

We'll discuss the airlines and the utilities. Other deregulating industries include insurance, railroads, and trucking. Available resources are being used to re-define markets and business strategies, not for e-commerce, new economy activities.

Airlines and Aerospace

The deregulation of the airlines was described in Chapter 5 as a mostly painful adjustment to competitive market realities. After a quarter century, the industry is finally nearing equilibrium although economic performance has been uneven. Consolidation for route and cost management may continue if the proposed UAL (United Airlines)/US Airways merger is approved by the Bush Administration.

Airline economics are driven by a multitude of factors, including business and leisure passenger traffic; freight shipment activity; the aging of the fleet; route structures; and access to commercial airport slots, gates, and maintenance facilities. While not directly regulated, the aerospace industry derives its demand from the requirements of the airline and from military sales, which in turn are a function of the geopolitical climate, the budgets of national governments, and lobbying.

E-commerce assists both industries: the airlines by support for procurement and some on-line ticketing; aerospace by improving inventory management and manufacturing systems. However, these industries experience their major expense pressures from labor and fuel costs, and may be reaching the limit to ticket price increases, particularly if the global economy softens.

---

[6] See the discussion in Chapter 7.

Exhibit 8-9: Airlines and Aerospace

Companies Ranked by Revenue	Companies Ranked by EPS Growth
Boeing	Lockheed Martin
Lockheed Martin	Textron
United Technologies	Cordant Technologies
Honeywell Intl.	Southwest Airlines
AMR	Precision Castparts
Raytheon	General Dynamics
UAL	UAL
Delta Air Lines	United Technologies
Textron	Honeywell Intl.
NWA	
Northrop Grumman	
General Dynamics	
Continental Airlines	
US Airways	

Airlines and aerospace companies ranked by revenue and growth in EPS are listed in Exhibit 8-9.

Utilities

The utility industry is regulated at the state level, with the result that any decision — as enabled by federal administrative rulings and legislation in the last decade — must be made at that level. Guidelines announced by the U.S. Energy Regulatory Commission in 1999 encourage the development of national power grids. It is anticipated that a national market for energy will eventually develop, allocating power to markets based on competitive bidding.

However, the current experience of California, the first state to deregulate its electric utilities, has not been positive. Rather than improvements in rates and service, prices have risen sharply and there have been a series of power blackouts. The situation there may be unusual in that California has consistently opposed the construction of new power facilities and controls the maximum price which can be charged, an inducement for producers to sell power in other markets.

In the absence of adequate power supplies and the construction of new generating facilities, e-commerce applications should provide moderate relief through the sale of energy through Internet bidding. Some websites are already in existence for that purpose.

Industry consolidation has been extensive. Recent gas and electric mergers include Virginia Electric and Power/Consolidated Natural Gas (2000), Dynegy/Illinois Power (2000), Wisconsin Electric Power/Wisconsin Gas (2000), Northeast Utilities/Yankee Gas (2000), and several others in the preceding years. Electric mergers include Consolidated Edison/Orange & Rockland (1999) and American Electric Power/Central and South West Corp.(1999). Other recent deals have involved financial transactions unusual in the industry, such as leveraged buyouts and acquisition of U.S. utilities by international companies.

Exhibit 8-10: Utilities

Companies Ranked by Revenue	Companies Ranked by EPS Growth
Duke Energy	Reliant Energy
PG&E Corp.	Nisource
Utilicorp United	DQE
Texas Utilities	Montana Power
Reliant Energy	Oneok
Southern	Duke Energy
Edison Intl.	Natural Fuel Gas
Entergy	Energy East
Avista	GPU
Consolidated Edison	PPL
American Electric Power	DPL
Unicom	Southern

Utilities ranked by revenue and growth in EPS are listed in Exhibit 8-10.

FINAL THOUGHTS ABOUT THE LOSERS

The "losers" represent a variety of industries struggling to compete in the changing environment of the early 21st century. Ironically, some of the companies represented in these industries were among the giants early in the last century. U.S. Steel and General Motors are two examples of formerly preeminent organizations that could not respond to product and service innovation and changing technology.

Investors have factored this deteriorating position into the valuation for these companies.

- The stock price of U.S. Steel (now USX) declined 57% in 2000, earnings fell an average of 11.7%, and the P/E was recently 9 times.

- The stock price of General Motors declined 32% in 2000, earnings rose an average of only 2.8%, and the P/E was recently 5 times.

In contrast, publicly-held companies experienced a 3% stock price increase in 2000, earnings rose an average of 3.6%, and the market's P/E was recently 25 times.

The losers also includes companies in industries which have been highly regarded by investors.

- There were 17 (of 53 reported) retailers trading at P/Es greater than 20 times earnings (as of year-end 2000), despite concerns for the continuation of general economic growth and an industry stock price decline in 2000 of 18%!

- Notwithstanding the weakness in commodity prices, 13 (of 26 reported) agribusiness companies traded at greater than 20 times earnings, and 12 sold at a greater stock price-to-book value than all publicly-traded companies![7]

"Loser" industries are still popular with investors, even though these companies and their managements will find it difficult to show superior performance in the developing e-commerce, new economy. We don't need them in our portfolios.

---

[7] These statistics are derived from "2001 Investment Outlook Scoreboard," *Business Week*, December 25, 2000, pages 138-174. Earnings percentage changes are for the 1995-1999 period.

Part III

A Portfolio for a Lifetime

The prudent man looketh well to his going.
The Holy Bible: The Old Testament, *Proverbs, 14:15*

Part I of this book discussed why financial results don't matter. Part II described our process for discovering the big winners, the moderate winners, and the losers in stock selection. Part III presents a procedure for thoughtfully constructing an investment portfolio focused on the twin essentials of liquidity and growth: liquidity for life's surprises and emergencies, and growth to develop the assets needed to assure a satisfying personal lifestyle.

We return to Jane Smith, and develop a plan for investing over a 30-year period using assumptions concerning her needs and her risk profile. To accommodate varying attitudes toward risk we establish three profiles: risk averse, risk tolerant, and risk accepting. We then show model stock portfolios for each risk profile and possible results over the investment period.

We use the concept of Beta described in Chapter 1 in our discussion of the efficient market hypothesis. Beta is a measure of the risk of an individual stock. When applied to old and new economy stocks, Beta produces the very interesting result that investors can achieve greater returns with less risk by focusing on the big winners than on the moderate winners. However, we attempt to construct a portfolio which is prudent, that is, which accommodates Jane's liquidity and investment growth needs.

Chapter 9

The Asset Segment Approach to Investing

Have I not walked without an upward look
Of caution under stars that very well
Might not have missed me when they shot and fell?
It was a risk I had to take — and took.
Robert Frost, *1874-1963 (American poet, from Bravado)*

An investment strategy oriented to old and new economy winners sounds like a great theory. In practice the winners may take time to stake out their positions, may spend more than originally budgeted on their e-commerce strategy, and may be exposed to any of an almost unlimited number of risks. However, investing is never riskless, unless you own only U.S. Treasuries (assuming that the federal government does not repudiate its debt).

In the meantime, you have to prudently construct an investment portfolio of stocks and other assets. To help you do this, the final chapter summarizes our approach to stock selection, and discusses the construction of an investment portfolio for investors with varying risk profiles.

INVESTMENT PLANNING

The approach to stocks discussed in Part II of this book focuses on the warriors and the wounded in the ongoing transition to the demands of business in the 21st century. This is very different from fundamental or technical analysis, and rejects the efficient market hypothesis. Instead, we are picking stocks using a methodology which focuses on adjustments to market pressures by established companies in the old and new economies.

Jane Smith's Situation

But ... we don't just want to pick some stocks. We want to construct a portfolio which will prudently build wealth. To do this, let's return to Jane Smith, introduced in Chapter 1. She is a 35-year old professional earning $50,000. After taxes and living expenses, she may have $5,000 per year to invest, which we expected would grow as her income increases.

We calculated that the after-tax value through the presumed age of retirement of 65 would be about $1.5 million, after paying some taxes on capital gains during the period. This outcome requires a 14% annual return. How should Jane plot her investment strategy to actually have a $1.5 million investment portfolio?

Stock market decisions are an integral component of the investor's total financial plan. A plan encompasses savings, financial investments, insurance, real estate, a will, and other elements. The idea behind planning is to allow the investor to increase his or her control over the uncertainty of such life events as marriage, child bearing, divorce, and retirement.

Jane's Life Events

Nearly every personal finance planner considers the question of how much Jane needs to finance her life events. Some advisors take an ultra-prudent investment strategy approach to the entire issue of investing, focusing on risk avoidance and the conservation of capital. The rationale is that the investor cannot easily replace any wealth lost through a portfolio decline.

However, risk avoidance does not provide much accommodation for those large expenditures necessary for a desired lifestyle, such as a house or higher education. It certainly does not support discretionary spending for life's indulgences, such as a vacation home or a luxury car, or for gifts to children for higher education or their first home, or for significant charitable contributions.

We are attempting to assist Jane to attain her lifestyle requirements for her earnings years and her post-earnings years. To do this, we need to be as aggressive as possible while assuring access to cash for emergency needs by assessing the investor's reasonable expectations from her savings and investments.

An appropriate place for Jane to begin investment decision-making is to calculate her personal financial statements:

- Her net worth, or the value of her assets, the things she owns, less her liabilities, the things she owes, which shows the net status of those amounts.

- Her cash flow, or her income less her expenses including regular living costs and payments on outstanding debt, to indicate the extent of potential investment and savings.

These calculations indicate the initial funds available for investing and the expected incremental amount from new net cash flow. How should these funds be invested?

One personal finance strategy is to focus on the "time horizon approach" to investing. Typically, recommendations are made based on likely requirements for each projected period of time. Possible short, medium, and long-term goals are listed in Exhibit 9-1.

Exhibit 9-1: Investment Goals by Time Range

Short-Term Goals

Reduce credit card, installment, and student loan debt
Begin savings program including contingency funds
Purchase term life insurance
Start fund for house downpayment

Medium-Term Goals

Diversify investments to include stock and mutual funds
Contribute to retirement savings plan (IRA or 401k)
Initiate separate savings programs for children
Save for major expenses (college tuition, vacation, automobile)

Long-Term Goals

Acquire retirement property
Develop sufficient investments to fund retirement
Purchase supplemental health and long-term care insurance
Develop estate plan including will, trusts, and lifetime gifts

The Asset Allocation Approach

Asset allocation typically manages the problem by considering alternative investments for Jane's available funds. The investor's focus is on the size of each major segment, usually stocks, bonds, and cash or money market instruments. The decision as to segment size or percentage is often based on an economic forecast, primarily the direction of interest rates and inflation. This may be further calibrated to the individual life cycle situation or time horizon.

For example, in periods of somewhat difficult economic conditions, it may be suggested that a young family have 30% of their holdings in stocks, 50% in bonds, and 20% in cash. A family in the prime earnings years in such an economy might have a larger stock market position, say 50%, and commensurately smaller bond and cash positions, say 40% and 10% respectively. A family entering retirement (with adult children) might be more conservative with a portfolio of 10% stocks, 70% bonds, and 20% cash.

The mutual fund industry and some investment advisors have subdivided the choices into specialized asset groupings involving numerous investment classes. These include various international bond and equity markets including emerging economies, commodities, real estate, and other potentially risky, somewhat illiquid choices. The problem is that data on performance over an extended time period are very sketchy, and there is no proof of the validity of this approach given the risks involved.

Our Asset Segment Approach

We take a different, somewhat simpler approach to investment decisions in this book. Based on the data in Chapter 1 on returns on alternative stock and bond market investments, there are only two asset segments all rational investors should consider.

- A liquidity segment comprised of money market or corporate bond mutual funds.

- A stock portfolio segment consisting of stocks with the potential to be winners in the new century, as augmented by indexed stock mutual funds.

We are not discussing precious metals, real estate, or other assets in this book. There appears to be no logical *investment* reason to hold them in your portfolio. We stress the word "investment" because there may be a *personal* reason to hold such assets, such as the enjoyment of a second home or pleasure of fine art or jewelry.

As long as you rationally decide to spend (and not invest) your savings for personal reasons, these are entirely acceptable decisions. However, never pretend that an expenditure on any non-financial asset is an investment. Art, gold and silver, and real estate are not liquid, may lose substantial value at the time of sale, and often incur very substantial selling costs.

THE LIQUIDITY SEGMENT

Every investor should have a liquidity segment for contingencies during times of emergency (such as a hospitalization) or stress (such as the breakup of a marriage). For most investors, the size of the liquidity segment should be three to six months of income. We're going to assume Jane Smith will need $20,000 (or about five months worth), an amount which will rise with increases in Jane's income.

In making this decision, it is not wise to be overly conservative, but to thoughtfully consider the *opportunity cost* of foregoing other investments. "Opportunity cost" is the consideration of alternative uses for capital currently invested or being considered for investment. The investor must always consider the various choices available and what their costs, returns, and risks are likely to be.

The size of the liquidity segment depends on such factors as the amount of the fixed obligations of the investor — for example, rent or mortgage payments, income and property taxes, education, medical care, etc. The larger the amount of these fixed obligations, the greater the liquidity segment should be. For example, if Jane rents an apartment and has limited credit card debt, she can get by on three months of income. If she owns a house, owes money on her educational and/or auto loans, and has dependents, she should accumulate six months of income.

Money Market Funds and Short-Term Investments

The ability to access liquid funds when needed with the principal intact is of paramount importance, rather than waiting for a maturity date or a distress sale. We recommend money market funds and bond funds for this purpose. Money market funds are mutual fund investments of liquid, short-term debt instruments. Bond funds are described in the next section.

The advantage of any money market investment is safety and current income, with a high probability that the principal invested will be available upon the maturity or liquidation of the investment. Assets held by money market funds include the safest instruments: U.S. Treasury obligations, repurchase agreements, bank CDs, commercial paper, and bankers acceptances; for definitions see Exhibit 9-2. The average yield on money market funds has been about 5% for the past decade.

There are various types of money market funds to consider. As with any investment, the choice depends largely on the degree of risk associated with each asset category held by the fund. Most mutual fund families[1] offer several short-term funds with varying asset quality, including a fund holding only U.S. government securities; one holding U.S. governments, agencies and derivative instruments (such as repurchase agreements); and one holding those instruments and the commercial paper issued by corporations. As noted in Exhibit 9-3, the slight difference in risk is reflected by the different returns offered by each fund.[2]

Exhibit 9-2: Descriptions of Short-Term Debt Instruments (Commonly Held in Money Market Funds)

Repurchase agreements (repos) – A holder of securities sells these securities to an investor with an agreement to repurchase them at a fixed price on a fixed date. The security "buyer" effectively lends the "seller" money for the period of the agreement. Most repos are overnight.

U.S. Treasury bills – The most liquid money market security, issued in short maturities, and backed by the full faith and credit of the U.S. government. Other forms of U.S. Treasury obligations include notes (with original maturities of 2 to 10 years) and bonds (with maturities of 10 to 30 years).

Bank certificates of deposit (CDs) – Issued by commercial banks and purchased by money market funds in jumbo amounts, with face values of $100,000 or more. The creditworthiness of the issuer is the security for the CD. Other forms of this instrument include Eurodollar CDs, issued by European branches of U.S. banks; and Yankee CDs, issued by U.S. branches of foreign banks.

Bankers acceptances (BAs) – Similar to bank CDs in that they are irrevocable obligations of the issuing bank. BAs are created to finance international trade, but are often sold by their holders to generate liquidity for internal operations.

Commercial paper – Issued by large corporate borrowers and backed by the creditworthiness of the issuer. An alternative mechanism for borrowing that is usually less costly and more flexible than bank loans.

---

[1] A mutual fund family is a group of funds managed by a single fund management company, such as Fidelity, T. Rowe Price, or Putnam.

[2] Betas, defined in Chapter 1, are not assigned to debt instruments or funds, so we use a surrogate Beta later in our illustrative portfolios (Exhibit 9-7) to represent varying risk levels.

Exhibit 9-3: Money Market Funds

Typical Name or Designation	Risk Level[a] and Surrogate Beta[b]	Typical Types of Instruments Held	Typical Yield Difference[c]
U.S. Treasury Fund	Essentially No Risk[d]/0.0	U.S. Treasury securities	
U.S. Government Fund	Minimal Risk/0.3	U.S. Treasury securities; U.S. agency securities[e]	+ 20-25 bp
Money Market Fund	Slight Risk/0.6	U.S. Treasury securities and agency securities; short-term debt issued by creditworthy international issuers, including financial institutions and governments	+ 40-50 bp

Notes:

[a] All debt instruments are subject to interest rate risk.

[b] Used in Exhibit 9-7

[c] Incremental yield from the funds with the "U.S. Treasury Fund" (the funds with the least risk) to the designated funds. "Bp" (basis points) is equivalent to 1/100th of one percentage point.

[d] Unless the U.S. Government repudiates its debt obligations

[e] U.S. agency securities may not be backed by the full faith and credit of the U.S. government

Exhibit 9-4: Bond Credit Ratings

Bonds rated "AAA" and "AA" differ only in a small degree, with both ratings signifying that the issuer can meet its financial commitments. An "A" rating is strong but somewhat more susceptible to the adverse effects of changes in circumstances and economic conditions. "BBB" signifies adequate protection parameters although adverse factors could lead to a weakened capacity of the issuer. Obligations rated "BB," "B," "CCC," "CC," and "C" have significant speculative characteristics.

Bond Funds

Bond funds are investments in long-term debt obligations of corporations or governments. There is significant variation in bond fund safety (or default risk) and maturity, with some funds offering the highest quality corporate debt (AAA and AA rated), and some mixed with lower credit ratings (A and BBB). For an explanation of these terms and other debt instrument concepts, see Exhibit 9-4. Because of the time to maturity (as much as 30 to 50 years), there can be substantial variation in the value of the bond fund.

As with any debt instrument, there is a direct inverse relationship between interest rates and bond prices. The only guarantee is that the bond will pay the contractual amount of interest due, and that the principal amount will be repaid at maturity, assuming the issuer is solvent. The investor seeking to avoid risk could focus on short-term portfolio maturities, while the investor who accepts risk might consider longer maturities. The risk arises from interest rate fluctuations while the investment is held; an increase in interest rates causes a proportional decline in the price of bonds, which in turn would affect the value of the fund's holdings.

U.S. government bond funds yielded about 5.5% (in early 2001), high quality bond funds (mostly AA) yielded 6.0% to 6.5%, lower quality bond funds (mostly BBB) yielded about 6.5% to 7.0%, and the average corporate bond fund returned 6.3% (for the year 2000). These yields are quoted on a "current yield" basis. An alternative yield is the yield-to-maturity, which is a present value calculation of the total of all interest and principal payments expected to be received by the bond's maturity.

Advantages of Money Market and Bond Funds

Money market and bond mutual funds are popular today because of several factors:

- *Accessibility.* A mutual fund combines investments from many participants into a pool of money to allow the purchase of securities. This pooling effect allows the smaller investor (with say $1,000) to participate in a diversified portfolio where the minimum purchase requirement is fairly large (usually $10,000). In other words, a $1,000 mutual fund investor gains the same diversification that a $250,000 direct investor would achieve. Furthermore, the buying clout of a mutual fund manager provides access to the best pricing for securities at the least transaction cost.

- *High yield.* Money market funds yield about 1% more than comparable bank savings products, due in part to the imposition of a "required reserve" on savings products of 3% by the Federal Reserve Board. (The "required reserve" is a portion of your deposit or investment set aside as non-interest bearing.) In addition, money market fund rates are set competitively by the action of the markets, while bank instruments are managed rates set to attract or dissuade deposits. Bond fund yields are equivalent to the yields on the underlying securities.

- *Convenience.* Nearly all money market and bond funds offer check writing privileges to access the amount invested, although there may a minimum check size or a limit on the number of checks which can be written. The convenience extends to telephone or Internet switching to other funds in the same mutual fund "family," should investment goals or economic views change.

- *Interest Crediting.* Interest is earned and credited daily in many money funds, and monthly for most bond funds, with posting monthly. There is usually no penalty or waiting period if you desire access to your money, and many funds will wire transfer a time critical withdrawal, such as a downpayment on a house.

- *Fund Expense.* Money funds have very low expenses, with the typical charge of ½ of 1% for management fees, marketing, and auditing. These fees are deducted from the interest (called "dividends") paid to the investor.

THE STOCK PORTFOLIO SEGMENT

Once provision for the liquidity segment has been made, the balance of the investment portfolio should be in stock market investments. The asset allocation problem, in our view, actually is a *stock market* allocation problem, with choices to be made among the following alternatives:

- Companies in industries which will be big winners in the new economy, as described in Chapter 6.

- Companies in industries which provide the infrastructure for the new economy, as discussed in Chapter 7.

- A basket of companies which match the performance of a specified market *index*.

Indexing

An index fund is a portfolio of assets constructed to match a benchmark average, most commonly the Standard & Poor's 500 (S&P 500) index. The fund managers attempt to duplicate the average by holding the same proportion of securities that are in the benchmark. Changes only occur if the composition of the benchmark changes, that is, if the index adds or drops a stock.

The same advantages of money market and bond funds apply to stock index funds, including professional management, diversification, a large selection of types of funds from which to choose, and a small initial investment requirement. In addition, many stock index funds have relatively stable holdings, or a more-or-less buy-and-hold strategy, leading to minimal capital gain distributions to investors and few taxes for those investors to pay.[3]

Because the management of the fund is passive, management fees are typically much lower than actively managed funds. Funds where decisions are made regarding purchases and sales charge about 1% of asset value for funds without sales charges (no load funds), and about 1.5% for funds with sales charges (load funds). In contrast, charges for index funds average about one third of 1%, or three to four and one-half times less.

Business Week reports that stock index funds consistently outperformed actively managed equity funds for the entire 1994-1998 period. Fewer than 5% of actively managed stock portfolios outperformed the Standard & Poor 500, and compounded index fund results exceed about 80% of managed stock investments. A principal contributor to these superior results is the lower fee structure in indexing, by some 1% of assets under management.[4] The advantages of higher returns and lower fees have caused a surge in index fund popularity, with 10%-15% of the annual flow of $200-$250 billion of mutual funds now placed in these investments.

---

[3] For further information on index funds, see Jerry Tweddell and Jack Pierce, *Winning with Index Mutual Funds*, AMACOM, 1997.

[4] "With Index Funds, Who Needs Gurus?" *Business Week*, January 18, 1999, pp. 108-110.

Exhibit 9-5: Stock Index Funds
(Using the S&P 500 as the Benchmark)[a]

Name of Fund[b]	Annualized 3-Year % Return[c]	Assets ($ Millions)	Load (L)/ No Load (NL)[d]	Expense Ratio (%)[e]
S&P 500 Ix.	12.3%			
BlackRock Ix. Equity	11.5	$2,026	L	0.75%
Dreyfus S&P 500 Ix.	11.7	3,075	NL	0.50
Eclipse Ix'd Equity	12.2	1,503	NL	0.30
Fidelity Spartan	12.1	10,187	NL	0.20
First American Index	11.6	1,690	L	0.60
MainStay Equity Ix.	12.6	1,233	L	0.95
Munder Ix. 500	11.7	1,449	L	0.45
One Group Equity Ix.	11.7	2,754	L	0.60
T. Rowe Price Equity Ix. 500	12.0	4,452	NL	0.40
SsgA (State Street Bank) S&P 500 Ix.	12.1	2,852	NL	0.20
USAA S&P 500 Ix.	12.1	3,340	NL	0.20
Vanguard 500 Ix.	12.3	104,358	NL	0.20

[a] In addition, there are several special purpose index funds, including Citizens Index Retail, Schwab Small Cap Index, and several Vanguard funds, including Extended Market Index, Growth Index, Mid Cap Index, Small Cap Index and Value Index. Index funds with less than three years of returns history and $1.0 billion in assets are excluded from this exhibit. There are several new funds, including: Armada Equity Index, Evergreen Equity Index, Fidelity 4-in-1 Index Fund of Funds, T. Rowe Price Total Equity Market Index, and perhaps a dozen funds with under $1.0 billion in assets.

[b] Ix. = Index

c For the years 1998-2000. The 3-year returns are obtained from the Spring 2001 issue of *Kiplinger's Mutual Funds 2001*.

[d] "Load" funds charge a sales fee for purchasing shares; "no load" funds do not charge a sales fee. The load charge is typically paid to a broker or sales agent as a commission. No load funds are purchased directly from the sponsoring organization.

[e] % of a fund's assets charged for management fees and other expenses

---

Exhibit 9-5 displays the largest stock index funds with recent statistics on size, three-year returns, sales charges (loads), and management fees. Vanguard, which pioneered the concept of an index fund, is by far the largest index fund family. Vanguard charges a nominal management fee and the fund has matched the performance of the S&P 500 (12.3% for the three-year period 1998-2000). Other funds may have a load charge and typically do slightly worse than the benchmark due to a higher management fee.

JANE'S INVESTMENT PROGRAM

To accumulate the targeted $20,000 of liquid holdings, Jane should begin allocating half of her annual investment contribution to the liquidity segment, or $2,500 to liquidity and $2,500 to stocks. Given the very significant difference in yield between money market funds and bond funds, there is a compelling reason to put as much as is prudent of the liquidity portion in longer-term securities.

Exhibit 9-6: Illustrative Liquidity/Stock Portfolio
(Based on 5% interest on a $1,000 Money Market Fund and 7.5% interest on a $1,500 Bond Fund[a])

Year	Money Market and Bond Fund Accumulation[b]	Stock Index Fund and Stock Accumulation[c]	Total After-Tax Accumulation
1	$2,630	$2,815	$5,445
2	$5,226	$5,985	$11,211
3	$10,384	$9,554	$19,937
4	$20,632	$13,573	$34,205
5	$21,705	$20,913	$42,618
6	$22,834	$29,178	$52,012
7	$24,021	$38,484	$62,505
8	$25,270	$48,963	$74,233
9	$26,584	$60,762	$87,347
10	$27,967	$74,048	$102,015
15	$36,035	$170,227	$206,262
20	$46,430	$344,316	$390,746
25	$59,825	$659,427	$719,251
30	$77,083	$1,229,794	$1,306,877

[a] Interest rate assumptions are derived from averages from the 1980-2000 period presented noted in Chapter 1.

[b] Assumes 5% interest on the money market portion and 7.5% interest on the bond fund portion, less federal and state taxes calculated at an effective rate of 20%. No new allocation is made after year 4.

[c] Assumes 14% growth on both index and specific stocks less taxes on 10% of the amount of the stock appreciation comprised of dividends and capital gains.

The risk in this strategy is that interest rates could rise, reducing the market value of the bond fund holdings. (Recall that there is an inverse relationship between interest rates and bond prices.) However, the slight inflation rate currently experienced in the U.S. does not make this a major concern. Remember also that mutual funds families allow Jane to allocate relatively small amounts (usually $1,000) to different types of investments.

Getting Jane Started

Jane should begin with $1,000 in a money market fund and $1,500 in a bond fund. Assuming no significant change in her financial situation, Jane would amass $20,000 in about the fourth year (see Exhibit 9-6). We assume that Jane has no income other than her $50,000 salary, takes the standard deduction,[5] and the one exemption[6] for herself of $2,550. This results in a federal tax of $9,053, an effec-

---

[5] The "standard deduction" is an amount deducted from "adjusted gross income" (AGI) in lieu of itemizing allowable deductions for such personal expenses as charitable contributions, mortgage interest and property taxes on a primary residence, and medical expenses which exceed 7.5% of AGI. The standard deduction amount in 2000 is $4,400 for single taxpayers and $7,350 for married taxpayers filing jointly.

[6] "Exemptions" are amounts allowed to taxpayers as a deduction for him/herself, a spouse, and each dependent supported by the taxpayer. There are several tests which determine if a dependent can be claimed. The exemption amount in 2000 is $2,800.

tive rate of about 18%. We also assume an effective 2% for state taxes. (For further information on tax calculations, see any standard tax reference.)

While it is prudent for Jane to amass $20,000 in the liquidity segment of her assets, it would force her to forego the appreciation potential from stock market investing. Jane should be comfortable with her financial situation, but should not choose a conservative strategy without considering the opportunity cost of that decision (as discussed earlier in this chapter). We recommend that the other $2,500 available to invest should be used initially to purchase a stock index fund.

The Betas of Old and New Economy Stocks

In Chapter 1 we described Beta and how a stock's price would be expected to fluctuate relative to the general stock market index (such as the S&P 500 index) based on its Beta. The general market has a Beta of 1.0. A Beta less than 1.0 indicates that a stock is less volatile than the general market as measured over time; a Beta greater than 1.0 indicates fluctuation greater than the market.

The big winners (discussed in Chapter 6) have an average Beta of just under 1.0 (0.95) and moderate winners (reviewed in Chapter 7) have an average Beta of well over 1.0 (1.17), a difference of nearly 20%! The volatility of the information sector stocks[7] drives this result, versus the relative stability of the old and new economy stocks expected to be the big winners.

This is a significant issue for investors. You will beat the market with less risk by investing in the big winners, rather than in either the general market or the high technology and financial stocks which led the markets in the most recent expansion. Since it's a win-win situation, it is worth repeating: your best strategy — investing in the big winners — has more potential reward and less risk (as measured by Beta) than any other investment strategy.

Risk Preference

We have not previously addressed capital allocation, the assignment of investable funds to specific asset segments. The capital allocation decision is a function of the risk preference of the investor. In our example, how much risk should Jane Smith accept in structuring her portfolio? This is a highly personal decision which is not subject to mathematical formulae or computer modeling.

We could look toward Beta, but saying we're a 1.0 or a 1.5, or risk averse or risk accepting overly simplifies a complex issue. The four questions that Jane (and you) should be considering are investment period, future income, debt obligations, and responsibility for dependents.

> • *Investment Period.* We discussed investment period concerns earlier in this chapter and provided specific goals for various time periods (see

---

[7] Some examples of these Betas: Compaq Computer, 1.25; Sun Microsystems, 1.25; Dell, 1.30; Silicon Graphics, 1.30; Computer Associates, 1.60; Oracle, 1.70; Texas Instruments, 1.70; SCI Systems, 1.75; Analog Devices, 2.25.

Exhibit 9-1). The longer the period, generally the more risk you can accept because of the future opportunity to replace any investment lost due to a price decline. For example, if retirement is a few years away, invest cautiously; if it's 25 years away, you can afford to take some risk.

- *Future Income.* Uncertain or level future income requires prudence with your investments, while the expectation of rising wages or salary allows you to consider some risk assumption.

- *Debt Obligations.* Owing considerable debt requires a conservative attitude toward risk, at least until a substantial portion of that debt is repaid. Otherwise, your credit rating could be jeopardized. Debts comfortably financed by current earnings allows more assumption of risk.

- *Dependents.* Single people or marrieds with no children or dependent parents can assume more risk than families with educational and other dependent expenses.

These are not categories which can be summed or weighted to arrive at a decision on your risk profile. Each must be considered independently and with full cognizance of your personal situation. If you won't sleep at night worrying about your 1.25 Beta portfolio, the solution is to stay with 0.75 or 1.0 Beta portfolios.

Jane and Her Sisters

We will assume several Jane Smiths, identical in every way except for different tolerances for risk.

- Jane #1 is averse to risk, unwilling to chance any of her savings on speculation. In that situation, her target portfolio Beta might be 0.75, deliberately underperforming the general stock market but not likely to lose much value in an economic downturn.

- Her twin sister Jane #2 is tolerant of risk, willing to accept some speculation in her portfolio to match the overall performance of the market. She may assume that the average market return would best meet her long-term investment strategy. Her target portfolio Beta would be 1.00.

- If they were triplets, Jane #3 might be eager to accept risk, hoping to find the next Enron or Wal-Mart. Her target portfolio Beta might be 1.25 to outperform the market in rising markets. This book is focused primarily on the goals of Jane #3, and any other investor seeking superior returns with acceptable risk.

The resulting allocation by segment is shown for our three Janes in Exhibit 9-7.

Exhibit 9-7: Portfolio Segments for Varying Risk Tolerance

Investor and Risk Tolerance	Jane #1 Risk Averse		Jane #2 Risk Tolerant		Jane #3 Risk Taking	
	Target Beta	Portfolio %	Target Beta	Portfolio %	Target Beta	Portfolio %
Liquidity[a]	0.0	25%	0.3	20%	0.6	15%
Indexed Stock Fund	1.0	30%	1.0	20%	1.0	10%
Big Winner Stocks	0.9	30%	1.2	40%	1.3	50%
Moderate Winner Stocks	1.2	15%	1.3	20%	1.5	25%
Total of Portfolio Segments		100%		100%		100%
Target Portfolio Beta	0.75		1.00		1.25	
Actual Portfolio Beta		0.75		1.00		1.25

[a] Beta is a not a concept calculated for liquidity segment investments. It is used here to represent the level of risk assumed by the investor.

Other personal finance advisors and investment managers may naively assume that Janes #1, #2, and #3 should have the same portfolio as they have the same personal situations. This is an obviously unrealistic assumption given their varying attitudes toward risk.

IMPLEMENTING THE ASSET SEGMENT APPROACH

Remember that the risk profile of any of the Janes determines the selection of specific investment choices. Risk aversion suggests a portfolio Beta of 0.75; risk tolerance, a portfolio Beta of 1.0; and risk acceptance a portfolio Beta of 1.25. Model portfolios are provided for each risk profile in Exhibit 9-8.[8] Six big winner and four moderate winner stocks are included, consistent with our preference for the higher reward and lower risk of the big winner industries.

Some restrictions to note:

- Liquidity should be a primary concern until the target of three to six months of income is attained.

- The indexed stock fund will always have a Beta of about 1.0, by definition.

- Old and new economy companies will have some variation in their Beta risk, with an average of slightly under 1.0.

- Companies providing the new economy infrastructure will have significant Beta risks, exceeding the average stock by perhaps 15% to 20%.

---

[8] Betas are stable for only a brief period, and fluctuate as individual stock prices and the markets change. Any decision to invest in specific stocks should be made using recent Beta statistics. For Betas of specific stocks, see the sources listed in Appendix 2.

Exhibit 9-8: Model Stock Portfolios Based on Risk Tolerances

Big Winners	Beta	Industry[a]	Moderate Winners	Beta	Industry[a]
Jane #1					
Abbott Labs	0.70	Ph	Bank of New York	1.30	Bk
Air Prdcts & Chmcls	0.90	C	Bell South	0.50	NC&T
Clorox	0.90	S&C	Dell	1.30	C&OE
Cooper Tire	1.00	R&P	Texas Instruments	1.70	SC
Eaton	0.80	T&E			
Hasbro	0.90	L&E			
Average Beta	0.9		Average Beta	1.2	
Jane #2					
Applied Materials	2.30	S/PE	Bank of New York	1.30	Bk
Avery Dennison	0.90	C	Oracle	1.70	S&P
Cooper Tire	1.00	R&P	Silicon Graphics	1.30	C&OE
Humana	1.15	HC	Washington Mutual	0.90	DF
Kimberly-Clark	0.70	FPP			
Navistar Intl	1.25	T&E			
Average Beta	1.2		Average Beta	1.3	
Jane #3					
Applied Materials	2.30	S/PE	Bear Stearns	1.75	DF
Cooper Tire	1.00	R&P	McGraw-Hill	0.85	P&A
Humana	1.15	HC	Oracle	1.70	S&P
Navistar Intl.	1.25	T&E	SCI Systems	1.75	C&OE
Sherwin-Williams	0.95	C			
Weyerhauser	1.20	FPP			
Average Beta	1.3		Average Beta	1.5	

[a] Industry Codes:

Bk:	Banking
C:	Chemicals
C&OE:	Computers and Office Equipment
DF:	Diversified Financials
FPP:	Forest and Paper Products
HC:	Health Care
L&E:	Leisure and Entertainment
NC&T:	Network Communications and Telecommunications
P&A:	Publishing and Advertising
Ph:	Pharmaceuticals
R&P:	Rubber and Plastics
S/PE:	Scientific/Photographic Equipment
S&C:	Soaps and Cosmetics
S&P:	Software and Peripherals
T&E:	Transportation and Equipment

Jane's Portfolio

Our original Jane #1 would make her liquidity investments in a combination of money market and corporate bond funds, as discussed above. She would make her first $2,500 stock investment in an indexed stock fund, her next $5,000 in any of the Chapter 6 companies, and her third $2,500 in any of the Chapter 7 companies.

This investment cycle of $2,500/$5,000/$2,500 should be repeated through Jane's working years. We assume that the stock market returns would be an annual 14%. After 20 years, the portfolios would be worth nearly $400,000, and at her 30*th* year, the presumed conclusion of her working career, the total value would be in excess of $1.3 million.

By slightly increasing the stock market return to reflect the higher portfolio risk (Beta) accepted by the other Janes, the total value after 30 years grows to more than $1.5 million for Jane #2 and $1.8 million for Jane #3. No other change in investment strategy is involved for Janes #2 and #3: just accepting more portfolio risk and owning stocks producing higher returns. Exhibits 9-9 through 9-11 provide details of year-by-year accumulations for Janes #1, #2, and #3.

JANE'S INVESTING HOMEWORK

Several important factors are at work in helping Jane Smith attain her economic goals, but she must be disciplined to allow them to work for her. First, she must allow the power of compounding to increase her net worth by resisting the temptation to invade her investments for spending on non-essentials as compared to real emergencies. There's nothing wrong with taking a vacation or buying an automobile, but any purchase should be financed through a personal budget and not from savings.

Second, Jane must do her homework. New economy investments do not pop up on her television or call her on the telephone. She has to get comfortable with the Internet, with CD-ROM data bases, and with any business library resource she may wish to research. She must resist the temptation to listen to tips or advice from well meaning friends and relatives. Even if the advice is correct, it has to fit into Jane's particular risk profile and long-term investment strategy.

Third, Jane has to be comfortable with her risk profile. If she would lie awake at night worrying about a $10,000 decline in her portfolio, she should realize that she is not Jane #3. She may be #1 or #2 but only she knows. Investing is not gambling; it's a thoughtful process of assuring security in times of emergencies and for any period when you're not employed full-time. Jane should think hard about her attitude toward risk before investing a penny.

Fourth, Jane has to be honest about the concepts presented in this book. If she...

... doesn't understand present value,
... doesn't know how to read a balance sheet,

... is generally lost with all of the stock market jargon that has evolved over
the past century

... then she should step back and study this subject through a basic investment text
or even through a college-level course.

A last thought: The investment climate is getting more and more difficult.
However, huge opportunities await those who are willing to make the effort. We
hope that you and Jane Smith will be members of that selective group.

Exhibit 9-9: Year-by-Year Accumulations for Jane #1

	Money Market Fund	Money Market Interest	Bond Fund	Bond Fund Interest	Total Accumulation Pre-Tax	Taxable Income	Tax	After-tax Accumulation	Stock Market Fund	Stock Growth	Tax on Stock Sales	Stock Accumulation	Total Accumulation
1	$1,000	$50	$1,500	$113	$2,663	$163	$33	$2,630	$2,500	$350	$35	$2,815	$5,445
2	$1,000	$50	$1,500	$113	$5,293	$333	$67	$5,226	$5,315	$744	$74	$5,985	$11,211
3	$1,000	$50	$1,500	$113	$10,518	$673	$135	$10,384	$8,485	$1,188	$119	$9,554	$19,937
4	$1,000	$50	$1,500	$113	$20,902	$1,348	$270	$20,632	$12,054	$1,688	$169	$13,573	$34,205
5								$21,705	$18,573	$2,600	$260	$20,913	$42,618
6								$22,834	$25,913	$3,628	$363	$29,178	$52,012
7								$24,021	$34,178	$4,785	$478	$38,484	$62,505
8								$25,270	$43,484	$6,088	$609	$48,963	$74,233
9								$26,584	$53,963	$7,555	$755	$60,762	$87,347
10								$27,967	$65,762	$9,207	$921	$74,048	$102,015
11								$29,421	$79,048	$11,067	$1,107	$89,009	$118,430
12								$30,951	$94,009	$13,161	$1,316	$105,854	$136,805
13								$32,560	$110,854	$15,520	$1,552	$124,821	$157,382
14								$34,254	$129,821	$18,175	$1,817	$146,179	$180,432
15								$36,035	$151,179	$21,165	$2,117	$170,227	$206,262
16								$37,909	$175,227	$24,532	$2,453	$197,306	$235,214
17								$39,880	$202,306	$28,323	$2,832	$227,796	$267,676
18								$41,954	$232,796	$32,591	$3,259	$262,129	$304,082
19								$44,135	$267,129	$37,398	$3,740	$300,787	$344,922
20								$46,430	$305,787	$42,810	$4,281	$344,316	$390,746
21								$48,845	$349,316	$48,904	$4,890	$393,330	$442,174
22								$51,385	$398,330	$55,766	$5,577	$448,519	$499,904
23								$54,057	$453,519	$63,493	$6,349	$510,663	$564,719
24								$56,868	$515,663	$72,193	$7,219	$580,636	$637,504
25								$59,825	$585,636	$81,989	$8,199	$659,427	$719,251
26								$62,935	$664,427	$93,020	$9,302	$748,144	$811,080
27								$66,208	$753,144	$105,440	$10,544	$848,041	$914,249
28								$69,651	$853,041	$119,426	$11,943	$960,524	$1,030,175
29								$73,273	$965,524	$135,173	$13,517	$1,087,180	$1,160,452
30								$77,083	$1,092,180	$152,905	$15,291	$1,229,794	$1,306,877

Exhibit 9-10: Year-by-Year Accumulations for Jane #2

	Money Market Fund	Money Market Interest	Bond Fund	Bond Fund Interest	Total Accumulation Pre-Tax	Taxable Income	Tax	After-tax Accumulation	Stock Market Fund	Stock Growth	Tax on Stock Sales	Stock Accumulation	Total Accumulation
1	$1,000	$50	$1,500	$113	$2,663	$163	$33	$2,630	$2,500	$375	$38	$2,838	$5,468
2	$1,000	$50	$1,500	$113	$5,293	$333	$67	$5,226	$5,338	$801	$80	$6,058	$11,284
3	$1,000	$50	$1,500	$113	$10,518	$673	$135	$10,384	$8,558	$1,284	$128	$9,713	$20,097
4	$1,000	$50	$1,500	$113	$20,902	$1,348	$270	$20,632	$12,213	$1,832	$183	$13,862	$34,495
5								$21,705	$18,862	$2,829	$283	$21,409	$43,114
6								$22,834	$26,409	$3,961	$396	$29,974	$52,808
7								$24,021	$34,974	$5,246	$525	$39,695	$63,717
8								$25,270	$44,695	$6,704	$670	$50,729	$75,999
9								$26,584	$55,729	$8,359	$836	$63,253	$89,837
10								$27,967	$68,253	$10,238	$1,024	$77,467	$105,433
11								$29,421	$82,467	$12,370	$1,237	$93,600	$123,021
12								$30,951	$98,600	$14,790	$1,479	$111,911	$142,862
13								$32,560	$116,911	$17,537	$1,754	$132,693	$165,254
14								$34,254	$137,693	$20,654	$2,065	$156,282	$190,536
15								$36,035	$161,282	$24,192	$2,419	$183,055	$219,090
16								$37,909	$188,055	$28,208	$2,821	$213,443	$251,351
17								$39,880	$218,443	$32,766	$3,277	$247,932	$287,812
18								$41,954	$252,932	$37,940	$3,794	$287,078	$329,032
19								$44,135	$292,078	$43,812	$4,381	$331,509	$375,644
20								$46,430	$336,509	$50,476	$5,048	$381,937	$428,368
21								$48,845	$386,937	$58,041	$5,804	$439,174	$488,019
22								$51,385	$444,174	$66,626	$6,663	$504,138	$555,522
23								$54,057	$509,138	$76,371	$7,637	$577,871	$631,928
24								$56,868	$582,871	$87,431	$8,743	$661,559	$718,426
25								$59,825	$666,559	$99,984	$9,998	$756,544	$816,369
26								$62,935	$761,544	$114,232	$11,423	$864,353	$927,288
27								$66,208	$869,353	$130,403	$13,040	$986,715	$1,052,923
28								$69,651	$991,715	$148,757	$14,876	$1,125,597	$1,195,248
29								$73,273	$1,130,597	$169,590	$16,959	$1,283,227	$1,356,500
30								$77,083	$1,288,227	$193,234	$19,323	$1,462,138	$1,539,221

Exhibit 9-11: Year-by-Year Accumulations for Jane #3

	Money Market Fund	Money Market Interest	Bond Fund	Bond Fund Interest	Total Accumulation Pre-Tax	Taxable Income	Tax	After-tax Accumulation	Stock Market Fund	Stock Growth	Tax on Stock Sales	Stock Accumulation	Total Accumulation
1	$1,000	$50	$1,500	$113	$2,663	$163	$33	$2,630	$2,500	$400	$40	$2,860	$5,490
2	$1,000	$50	$1,500	$113	$5,293	$333	$67	$5,226	$5,360	$858	$86	$6,132	$11,358
3	$1,000	$50	$1,500	$113	$10,518	$673	$135	$10,384	$8,632	$1,381	$138	$9,875	$20,259
4	$1,000	$50	$1,500	$113	$20,902	$1,348	$270	$20,632	$12,375	$1,980	$198	$14,157	$34,789
5								$21,705	$19,157	$3,065	$307	$21,915	$43,621
6								$22,834	$26,915	$4,306	$431	$30,791	$53,625
7								$24,021	$35,791	$5,727	$573	$40,945	$64,966
8								$25,270	$45,945	$7,351	$735	$52,561	$77,832
9								$26,584	$57,561	$9,210	$921	$65,850	$92,435
10								$27,967	$70,850	$11,336	$1,134	$81,052	$109,019
11								$29,421	$86,052	$13,768	$1,377	$98,444	$127,865
12								$30,951	$103,444	$16,551	$1,655	$118,340	$149,291
13								$32,560	$123,340	$19,734	$1,973	$141,101	$173,661
14								$34,254	$146,101	$23,376	$2,338	$167,139	$201,393
15								$36,035	$172,139	$27,542	$2,754	$196,927	$232,962
16								$37,909	$201,927	$32,308	$3,231	$231,005	$268,914
17								$39,880	$236,005	$37,761	$3,776	$269,990	$309,870
18								$41,954	$274,990	$43,998	$4,400	$314,588	$356,542
19								$44,135	$319,588	$51,134	$5,113	$365,609	$409,744
20								$46,430	$370,609	$59,297	$5,930	$423,977	$470,407
21								$48,845	$428,977	$68,636	$6,864	$490,749	$539,594
22								$51,385	$495,749	$79,320	$7,932	$567,137	$618,522
23								$54,057	$572,137	$91,542	$9,154	$654,525	$708,582
24								$56,868	$659,525	$105,524	$10,552	$754,497	$811,364
25								$59,825	$759,497	$121,519	$12,152	$868,864	$928,689
26								$62,935	$873,864	$139,818	$13,982	$999,701	$1,062,636
27								$66,208	$1,004,701	$160,752	$16,075	$1,149,377	$1,215,586
28								$69,651	$1,154,377	$184,700	$18,470	$1,320,608	$1,390,259
29								$73,273	$1,325,608	$212,097	$21,210	$1,516,495	$1,589,768
30								$77,083	$1,521,495	$243,439	$24,344	$1,740,591	$1,817,674

Appendix 1

Strategies of Successful Investment Managers

Be not afraid of greatness: some are born great, some achieve greatness, and some have greatness thrust upon them.
William Shakespeare, *1564-1616 (Twelfth Night, act II, sc. v)*

The "efficient market hypothesis" assumes that an investor cannot select stocks which consistently outperform the stock market. The approaches of a dozen of the better known and more successful investors and collaborators are noted in this appendix. They have been generally acknowledged to outperform the equity markets in their stock selections, with annual returns regularly far exceeding those of general market averages. These individuals were operating at various times during the 20th century, and their approaches may no longer be relevant to the economic conditions of the 21st century.

WARREN BUFFETT

Buffett's approach has been to ignore macroeconomic forecasts, and buy those few stocks with a business franchise or a privileged position, allowing some immunity to competition. Examples include television stations, advertising agencies, newspapers, real estate companies, and situations where demand for the product or service is price inelastic (that is, where increases in price do not significantly affect the amount of product purchased). He avoids retailing, companies requiring huge research and development expenditures, agribusiness, and most highly financially leveraged companies, although he has taken major positions in two insurers, GEICO and General Reinsurance.

PAUL CABOT

Cabot managed Harvard University's endowment fund for nearly two decades after World War II, and was the founder and a partner in the State Street family of mutual funds. His investment approach to common stocks was conservative and cautious, emphasizing thorough research and investigation, realism toward economic opportunities, and industries with a strategic position and a relatively small labor-heavy technology component.

PHILIP FISHER

A leading California investment adviser, Fisher recommends long-term investing in outstanding businesses based on technology, not mass consumption, with characteristics of product sales growth, high profits, a leading position in its industry, and outstanding management. He looks for opportunities to buy at below the "intrinsic" value but does not sell when that level is attained due to capital gains taxes and the inevitable failure to re-purchase at a reasonable price. Fisher believes in a long-term perspective without concern for quarterly EPS or short-term problems (i.e., strikes, negative publicity, a major capital investment without immediate returns).

BENJAMIN GRAHAM AND DAVID DODD

The developers of value investing, Graham and Dodd believed that stocks should be sought whose intrinsic worth exceeded that of current equity valuations due to market inefficiencies. Graham's rules regarding stock investing, originally published in 1934, were as follows:

- Buy stocks for less than two-thirds of their net quick assets (working capital less all debt).

- The debt-to-equity ratio should be less than one.

- Earnings yield (the reciprocal of the P/E ratio) should be twice the prevailing AAA bond yield.

- Dividends yield should be greater than two-thirds of the AAA bond yield.

Lists of such stocks are regularly published in Standard & Poor's *Outlook*, the *Value Line Investment Survey,* and *Forbes Magazine*. This approach was claimed to average an annual appreciation of about 19% during the 50-year period of 1925-1975 versus an average annual appreciation of 3.5% for the DJIA.

PETER LYNCH

Peter Lynch and Warren Buffett are arguably the most recognized investment gurus of our time. No longer active in the management of the Magellan Fund, Lynch is primarily occupied with marketing for the fund's parent, Fidelity Investments. There is no overriding theme to Lynch's investment approach except for intensive research and analysis. He believes in taking broad positions in the industries he selects, and in subsequently weeding out the slower performers. He buys or sells quickly when predetermined price targets are reached, and consequently has a shorter time horizon than many other money managers. His goal is to find stocks with low P/Es, a 15%-20% ROE, and a strong business position. He generally avoids high technology and leading stocks in industries which are trendy speculations, and has little concern for managewent's policy on paying dividends.

JOHN NEFF

A classic "value" investor, Neff ran the Vanguard Windsor Fund for three decades. He focused on "underpriced" stocks which were temporarily in disfavor, and sold when the market price exceeded the intrinsic value. He was working at a time when dividend yield was still significant for many stocks, and he believed that such income was an important component of valuation. Neff focused on selected industries in which he developed expertise derived from detailed research including company field visits. His approach generally avoided the popular growth stocks with high market capitalizations.

T. ROWE PRICE

A mutual fund innovator, Price evolved a strategy to buy growth companies which reached a new price high at each business cycle peak, manifesting superior research and development, little competition, little governmental regulation, low labor costs, and a 10% ROE. He developed detailed rules for stock valuation based on P/E ratios, which generally involved not paying more than one-third over the lowest P/E the stock price reached during several market cycles.

RICHARD RAINWATER

Rainwater is a Texan who developed successful investment strategies while working for the Bass family of Fort Worth, whose fortune was based on oil. Now an independent investor, his primary focuses are energy, real estate, and healthcare. His role is unusual in that he actively participates as an administrator and investment banker, although always seeking to hire superior business managers. The general strategy is to target an industry in "disrepute," then find a company or sector within the industry with a sustainable competitive advantage or franchise. Rainwater invests with a few trusted partners, and uses financial leverage (borrowed capital) whenever possible.

JULIAN ROBERTSON

Robertson ran Tiger Fund from 1980 to 2000, when it was closed due to losses resulting from the pause in the long-term bull market. The Tiger Fund was a hedge fund, which took leveraged long positions offset by some short positions. Robertson was initially oriented to U.S.-based, well managed companies. He made his reputation by international positions in equities and currencies, in such regions as Europe, the Indian subcontinent, the Far East, and Central and South America.

GEORGE SOROS AND JIM ROGERS

Soros and Rogers are linked as the managers of the offshore Quantum Fund, although Rogers left active management in 1980. They were pioneers in the use of leverage to build large, hedged positions in various financial securities including currencies, and in the search for investment opportunities in overlooked countries in Africa, Asia, and Europe. They believe that the focus of most institutional money managers — economics and the business position — emphasizes the wrong investment factors, and that the proper orientation is on major secular changes. Their performance has been outstanding over time, although there have been some major losses from specific trading positions.

JOHN TEMPLETON

Templeton pioneered in finding stocks of non-U.S. companies in markets throughout the world, using an intrinsic value approach. Many of his stock selections are small, unknown companies of little interest to other investment advisers. He avoids companies subject to regulation, and tries to find investments in unregulated industries and those with natural monopolies in their market. The critical factors he examines are the P/E ratio, operating profit margins, liquidating value, and the earnings growth rate of the company, although he believes in flexibility rather than rules and formulas.

MARTIN ZWEIG

The Zweig Forecast has consistently been one of the top performing newsletters among investment advisory services. Zweig follows monetary policy through Federal Reserve actions and the movement of interest rates, and uses a variety of technical indicators to determine market sentiment (or to be on the right side of major market moves). Individual stocks are selected using P/E ratios, the trend of earnings, certain balance sheet items, and the price action of the stock.

Appendix 2
Sources of Investment Data

I am the very model of a modern Major-General.
I've information vegetable, animal, and mineral,
I know the Kings of England, and I quote the fights historical,
From Marathon to Waterloo, in order categorical.
Sir William S. Gilbert, *1836-1911 (Pirates of Penzance)*

The British composed some of the most biting satire on their own class system ever written. The "modern" military leader in *Pirates of Penzance*, Major General Stanley, is one of several pompous Gilbert and Sullivan characters who knows lots of useless information. As an investor, you are faced with the choice of using the same misleading data that analysts have used for generations, or with breaking new ground in the search for investment insights.

We have used the following sources in developing the information on companies and industries discussed in this book. In addition, company-specific Websites and published financial data were consulted, including annual financial reports and 10-K filings.

PART II SOURCES

The industry and company descriptions in Part II are derived from various sources, including the following:

Business Week, various issues including the annual survey of "America's Key Industries" published in the first week of each year (i.e., see the issue of January 8, 2001, pages 88 to 140); www.businessweek.com.

Fortune Magazine, various issues including the annual Fortune 500 published in mid-April (i.e., see the issue of April 17, 2000, pages 130 to 295 and F-1 to F82); www.fortune.com.

Hoover's Internet website, particularly "companies & industries"; www.hoovers.com.

S&P Industry Surveys, published in three volumes and updated semiannually by The McGraw-Hill Companies, New York NY; www.standardand-poors.com.

> *Value Line Investment Survey*, industry and company descriptions, financials and statistical data, published weekly by Value Line Publishing, New York NY; www.valueline.com.

The results which are reported are derived from financial data compiled for fiscal year 1999, with concentration data from census data. For census sources, see Exhibit 5-6.

PART III SOURCES

There are numerous sources on mutual fund performance, including dozens of Websites and periodicals. The following publications are available at some newsstands and many libraries:

> *Barron's*, "The Best Mutual Fund Families," Issue of February 5, 2001.

> *Forbes Magazine*, "Mutual Fund Ratings: Stock Funds," Issue of February 5, 2001.

> *Kiplinger's Mutual Funds 2001*, published by Kiplinger's Personal Finance.

> *Money Magazine*, special mutual fund survey issue, February 2001.

> *Morningstar Mutual Funds 500*, Morningstar Inc., Chicago IL, 2000. In addition, Morningstar publishes a semi-monthly update service.

> *Weiss Ratings' Guide to Stock Mutual Funds* and *Weiss Ratings' Guide to Bond and Money Market Mutual Funds,* A Thomson Financial Company, Rockville MD. In addition, Weiss publishes a quarterly update service.

> Wiesenberger Investment Companies Service, *Investment Companies Yearbook 2000*, A Thomson Financial Company, Rockville MD. In addition, Wiesenberger publishes a monthly update service.

> Gordon K. Williamson, *The 100 Best Mutual Funds You Can Buy*, Adams Media Corp., Holbrook MA 2000; published annually.

GENERAL SOURCES

Corporate financial information is reported by the business press, in filings with regulatory bodies (such as the Securities and Exchange Commission), and through issuance of periodic financial reports. The basic financial reporting document is the annual report, which presents a balance sheet, income statement and supplemental exhibits prepared by the company's external auditors (or accountants). The annual report is supplemented by statements of quarterly earnings.

The purpose of an independent report, rather than one developed by internal accounting, is to objectively present the financial position of the company as of the end of the reporting period. Although the annual report is the best source for company financial data, common practice is to consult the various print and electronic media which compile and arrange the data in a summary presentation.

The primary newspaper media are *The Wall Street Journal, The New York Times, Investor's Business Daily,* and *Barron's.* All four publications report quarterly earnings, strategy, and personnel changes, and other investment data. The important business magazines include *Fortune, Business Week,* and *Forbes.*

Financial manuals, handbooks, and services are published by various organizations, the most important of which include Standard & Poor's, Moody's, Value Line, Hoover's, and Bloomberg.

- *Moody's:* Now published by Mergent, the Moody's services include annual manuals for various groupings of companies. These include the Industrial company manual (red cover), the OTC (over-the-counter or NASDAQ listed) company manual (gray cover), the Bank & Finance manual (black cover), and the International company manual (blue cover). Mergent also publishes a quarterly service, the *Handbook of Common Stocks,* which includes one page summaries of publicly-traded stocks.

- *Standard & Poor's:* Provides a daily news service, with current earnings and management reports. S&P also provides a service of monthly stock reports. Most of S&P's product offerings focus on corporate and not-for-profit credit ratings, the publication of various indices of market performance, economic analyses, and the compilation of financial and statistical data.

- *Value Line:* Publishes a comprehensive, weekly service, *The Value Line Investment Survey,* covering 1,700 stocks and nearly 100 industries. Each stock is ranked for relative price performance in the coming year. Individual stock reports are presented including the company's past performance, current status, and outlook, along with industry reviews. The CD-ROM version allows integration with the company's Website.

- *Hoover's:* Hoovers is probably best known for its on-line data bases, previously noted, and its CD-ROM listings of public and private companies compiled by region. Their business press also annually publishes directories of companies, on such topics as American business, emerging companies, and international companies.

- *Bloomberg:* Provides business information through various media, including a news service, television, radio, magazines and a comprehensive Website (www.bloomberg.com). The Bloomberg Professional service is offered through a PC with information delivery and analysis 24 hours a day.

Index